# The Assault on Social Policy

# The Assault on Social Policy

William Roth

COLUMBIA UNIVERSITY PRESS    NEW YORK

COLUMBIA UNIVERSITY PRESS
*Publishers Since 1893*
*New York   Chichester, West Sussex*

Library of Congress Cataloging-in-Publication Data
Roth, William, 1942–
    The assault on social policy / William Roth.
        p. cm.
    Includes bibliographical references and index.
    ISBN 0-231-12380-9 (cloth : alk. paper)
    ISBN 0-231-12381-7 (pbk. : alk. paper)
    1. United States — Social policy — 1993–.
2.  Business and politics — United States.
3.  Corporations — United States — Political activity.
I. Title.
    HN65 .R66 2002
    361.6′1′0973 — dc21                    2001042142

Columbia University Press books are printed on
permanent and durable acid-free paper.
Printed in the United States of America
c  10  9  8  7  6  5  4  3  2  1
p  10  9  8  7  6  5  4  3  2  1

*For Three Women:*

*Carol Chisholm Roth*
*Evelyn Roth Fogarasi*
*Stefanie Zeimer Roth*

# Contents

# Foreword

In the United States today the wealthiest 1 percent of the population owns more than the bottom 95 percent. In this, the richest country in history, some 45 million Americans have no health insurance, and we have, by far, the highest rate of childhood poverty among economically advanced nations. Today, often under great stress, Americans work longer hours than do people in other industrialized nations while the system providing child care for their children is a disaster. In my state of Vermont, as throughout the country, many senior citizens are unable to afford the prescription drugs they need, because they have no Medicare prescription drug benefit and because the prices we pay for medications are the highest in the world. Further, far from being mended and extended, our social safety net is unraveling.

Frighteningly, in our country today more and more of our citizens are giving up on the political process. Indeed, the vast majority of poor people and young people do not participate in politics, and have no faith in it. Most young people in our schools are ignorant and misinformed about the most basic elements of the American political structure, or how to influence it. Meanwhile, the rich contribute massively and outrageously every year to both major political parties, and their lobbyists have enormous impact over decision making in Washington, D.C., including decision making on social policy.

Our media, which is heavily dominated by corporate interests, tells us what news we are supposed to consider important—in twelve-second sound bites. We hear, see, and read more than we ever wanted to know about O. J. Simpson and Bill Clinton's sex life, about fires, murders, and hurricanes— but we are told very little about the realities of life for the majority of people in this country. We are told we should care deeply about who wins the Super Bowl but not about how much control we should have over our lives. We have the "power" to decide which designer jeans we should buy but no power to stop our job from going to China or to ensure that we will receive adequate health care. We have "free choice" over what TV channel we watch but little choice about the horrendously long and stressful hours that so many of us have to work.

The Assault on Social Policy examines the usual suspects in a fashion that has become all too rare. Thus William Roth investigates poverty, welfare, health, and the Social Security system we will take up in Congress. He also examines less usual subjects like disability and children, which raises the question of why such issues have been customarily left to the margins of our debate. He considers the impacts of economics, politics, technology, corporations, the media, and globalization on our social policy. The lack of such consideration makes debate about social policy less meaningful and leads to a lesser likelihood of changing social policy for the better. Perhaps most important, Roth's book measures social policy against people and their rights and needs. That people should be the measure of social policy is obvious, but this perspective is disturbingly novel and refreshing.

Roth's excellent and provocative book, The Assault on Social Policy, addresses some of the major trends in American social and political life. And he approaches his subject from a strong bias: He firmly believes in democracy and the right of the people, not multinational corporations, to make the important decisions that affect our lives. He warns us about the growing influence of corporate America in almost every aspect of our society: politics, health care, education, Social Security, the media, and, importantly, on how we approach social policy in this country.

Roth focuses on questions of enormous consequence. Are the goals of social policy in this country to improve the lives of all people, or are they to increase the profit margins of the wealthy? Should the most important decisions affecting the men, women, and children of this country be made in open, democratic, and public debate, or should they be made behind the closed doors of large corporations? In a democratic, civilized society, what are each of us entitled to as human beings?

Roth has written an impressive book that should be read by every member

of Congress, by all students of social policy, and everyone else who is concerned about the future of this country and our basic institutions. He has
written a book that challenges us when he states that democracy means "rule
of civic society exercised of, by, and for the people. Such democracy is rare
and difficult to achieve, but it is hardly impossible. The liberty we expect is
hard to come by and requires constant vigilance, but liberty is also far from
impossible."

William Roth's book should be dissected and debated, which is what he
is asking us to do. At a time when wealthy corporate interests have more
power than they have ever had, we must undertake a thorough examination
of all aspects of our society, and struggle for ways to make our nation and
our globe more democratic and more just. This book will be a valuable tool
in that struggle.

*Representative Bernard Sanders*
*Member of Congress*
*Independent-Vermont*

# Acknowledgments

I have had the privilege of learning from many excellent teachers. In college and graduate school, none has been more influential than Charles E. Linblom. Among colleagues and contemporaries, no one has taught me more than Gary Saxonhouse. From the generation of my students, no one has made more of an impression than Daniel Roth. Nonetheless, the responsibility for this book is mine alone, and I absolve the people mentioned above, as well as those mentioned below, from any of it. Indeed, in this book, I have mild to profound disagreements with all.

I thank other friends and colleagues for their support, information, and criticism. They include Katharine Briar-Lawson, Shirley Jones, Hal Lawson, Irene Lurie, Bruce Miroff, Janet Perloff, and Brenda Smith. I thank Richard Sugarman for conveying to me some of his concern with reason and justice. I thank Sara Knapp for numerous discussions and cogent critique. I thank Bernard Sanders for his generous foreword and his public service. I thank John Michel, Irene Pavitt, Rita Bernhard, and the other people at Columbia University Press for their care and professionalism in transforming a manuscript into this book. The memory of the late Richard H. de Lone has been my constant companion.

I thank the numerous secretaries whose patience was exceeded only by their skill. They include Elizabeth Adamo, Cynthia Alexander, Diane Darbyshire, Erin Finnigan, Barbara Gabriel-Catalano, Margaret Pitta, and Lynn Razzano.

# The Assault on Social Policy

# Introduction

Times Square, the "Center of the World," has emerged from years of tawdriness into the new polish of digitally triggered billboard systems. Pornography and prostitution have slunk away. Bright multiplexes, worthy of the best suburban mall, have replaced dingy urban movie theaters. Mickey Mouse and other beloved Disney characters have taken over from the rats and roaches.

On December 31, 1999, the dramatic lowering of a new Waterford crystal ball marked the beginning of the third millennium. Predictions of Y2K terrorism never materialized at that happier time, because appropriate precautions had been taken; because, as was generally felt, there was less cause for fear; because of luck; or perhaps all the above. Despite what the more puritanical may have perceived as unruliness and lawlessness, most saw the revelry and flaunting of liquor laws as exuberance befitting the occasion, which is how the police, expecting the best but prepared for the worst, also seemed to perceive it.

In pre-millennium but post-television New Year's celebrations, the dropping of the ball at Times Square commemorates the new year even for those who are not present. Thousands watch TV as the ball descends and reaches its target destination. Distant gatherings and parties pause before the television set to see the ball drop.

What holds for any New Year held brilliantly for the singular New Year that marked the millennium, not least because of the revolution in telecommunication technologies that made worldwide celebrations of the new millennium transmissible for all to see (most excellently by CNN, whose twenty-four-hour news cycle, global reach, and transformation of local occurrences into global events have transformed Ted Turner, CNN founder, from an eccentric into a billionaire and visionary). The millennial inauguration was a fabulous demonstration of new technologies and their connection to us all. Countries from around the globe not only applauded the new millennium but celebrated it as a superbly choreographed TV event. (Only cynics could have regarded the occasion as an advertisement for third-millennial tourism.) People had their favorites, of course, such as the sound-and-light show at the Egyptian pyramids.

The change in millennium occurred at 12:00 A.M., December 31, 1999. It usually goes unnoticed that this marks not only a time but a combination of time and space (not to be confused with the time-space continuum of special relativity), midnight occurring every hour according to one's longitudinal position around the globe. Thus it took twenty-four hours for 12:00 A.M., December 31, 1999, to complete itself globally. This is significant given three factors: (1) global television; (2) nations around the globe preened in free air time; and (3) the change in millennia. The result was that the new millennium's first super event was a fabulous twenty-four-hour global television show.

Although this worldwide TV show was the best and the brightest of more than a thousand points of light around the globe, let us return, however reluctantly, to Times Square, which then found itself in a Manhattan undergoing change. To many, the remaking of the city was beneficial and long overdue: the transit systems were safer, people felt freer to walk the streets, the graffiti that once marred city walls had practically vanished. Manhattan and its visitors had taken back the night. For those who could afford it, shopping became exciting, and for those who could not, window shopping provided its own joy. Culture bloomed; the South Street Seaport, Tribecca, Soho, and other newly emergent neighborhoods joined Times Square as tourist attractions. Manhattan's wealth was enjoyed even by touring college students. Indeed, there evolved a "Manhattan Renaissance," for once again Manhattan was a tourist mecca, a focal point of culture, a global financial center, surely the appropriate place for a crystal ball to mark the new millennium.

Even at more sober moments more distant from the millennium, it was a brave new world for many people. Good jobs abounded. The days when jobs were in jeopardy in the face of lean and mean corporate downsizing were substantially over; most restructuring was a thing of the past, and that which remained had been accommodated into a new mind-set, a new lifestyle. Besides, why should corporate employers have felt any loyalty to their employees when the latter no longer felt loyal to them? The Dow crashed 11,000 before retreating; the NASDAQ soared above 5,000 before falling back through 2,000; and corporations had shared a piece of the action in the form of stock options, 401Ks, and the like, the government following suit with IRAs and college IRAs.

Use of the Internet became an open private perk, at least during lunch hour, when employees averaged some fifteen minutes observing and adjusting their investments. Given the fabulous escalation of the stock market, many people were rich. Even though salaries may not have increased, people felt free to spend, as they discovered what had traditionally been termed the "wealth effect," whereby rich people spend more of real or paper profits.

True, most people were likely to work some sixty hours a week, and their spouses were likely to be employed as well. But that allowed them to live in two-income dwellings where their children were physically safer and had more after-school activities to prepare them for college. Further, kids of course, like their parents, wanted designer clothes, expensive cars, and glamorous dates. While they certainly had a right to such luxuries, they were also obliged to work for them—and kids who worked were less likely to get into trouble. When employees got sick, employers provided good health insurance. Those employees astute enough to know that employers regard benefits as coming from the same pool as salaries were also wise enough to realize that the government kicks in some benefits by not taxing them. (If anything, taxes were too high anyway, a judgment the corporations shared.) Some may even have felt that they were living in the best of times, that things could only get better.

Not everyone felt so fortunate, however, at the dawn of the new millennium. Large areas around Times Square were cordoned off to traffic. One could pass through only by police escort. Some people remained in their offices after work to glimpse a view of the millennial events from a window, or, more commonly, many traveled there by subway. Among the revelers arriving by subway were those from the poorer fringes of Manhattan, the South Bronx, and Bedford Stuyvesant in Brooklyn, as well as poor people from areas less well known. Of course, these people did have money for the subway ride, were healthy enough to take it, and were willing to brave the walk between their residences and the nearest subway stop—stiff requirements even for a millennium. Nevertheless, many poor people were real-life witnesses to the dropping of the crystal ball.

With a national unemployment rate sufficiently low to make Alan Greenspan, chairman of the Federal Reserve Board, lose his hair, even low enough to have made the employment of new workers problematic for many corporations, many people who saw the ball drop were from areas where the level of unemployment exceeded 50 percent. They were from places where people had a low life expectancy, poor health, and poor education; where people contributed disproportionately to the 2 million occupying American prisons; in short, they were poor and oppressed. One mark of the new millennium was that the economic distance between the rich and the poor had never been so great. Another was that social policy was inadequate, underfunded, even in disrepute.

And what was the situation in Egypt and Africa, the country and continent that featured a favorite colossal event of those twenty-four hours signaling the new millennium, the sound-and-light show at the pyramids? Although both have their share of fabulously rich and powerful people, most of the population in Egypt and Africa are poor. Indeed, as in New York, never has the difference between haves—those who control capital and the corporate conglomerations of capital—and have-nots—those who have no such control—been so great. Further, the standard of living in Egypt and Africa has never been so distant from that in the United States. In short, the contrast between haves and have-nots has never been so great between rich and poor countries, within rich countries themselves, and within poor countries. These are not natural circumstances; they have been created by people.

At times grudgingly, at other times more bountifully, the world's developed countries use a small portion of the wealth and income of rich people and corporations to pay for various social policies that are largely targeted at poor people and designed to make the effects of modern capitalism less burdensome, sometimes even beneficial, to poor people. This is particularly true in countries that developed and prospered under industrial capitalism, such as the United States, Japan, and the countries of western Europe. The mechanism that implements such policies is commonly known as the welfare state. The United States stands out because of the remarkably late arrival of the welfare state to its shores.

The welfare state did not become a serious issue in the United States until President Franklin D. Roosevelt's New Deal. Dwight D. Eisenhower, the first Republican to become president since the New Deal, did not dismantle the welfare state—to the dismay of some in this party. Apparently, the welfare state and the social policy it embodied were above politics. Moreover, under President Eisenhower, not only did the welfare state endure but aspects of its social policy increased. Transfer payments under the Nixon administration put post-transfer poverty at a historic low. Thus, aside from modifications at the margin, social policy and the welfare state were substantially bipartisan.

Essentially the welfare state funds social policy through taxes. Several reasons have been advanced to explain the existence of social policy fulfilling at least some promise of a bountiful economy for all. Perhaps haves support social policy because they are good, generous, and caring people. Or perhaps social policy is provided only under the threat of violence or at least the threat of a noncooperative labor force. Or it may be that social policy emerges as a means of holding nations together, that it helps these nations define themselves, that indeed social policy is an adjunct to nationalism.

This book was written before the horrors of September 11. It has not taken them into account. Yet, if anything, these tragedies may have made its arguments even more important. Each of the following chapters deals with facets of social policy. The book is not meant to be an exhaustive examination of social policy, nor is it bipartisan, nonpartisan, or even impartial. As will also become evident, the conviction addressed here is that current social policy is inadequate, undemocratic, even disgraceful. Indeed, it is the author's belief that the start of this brave new millennium has been accompanied by a crisis that demands rapid changes and realistic, "big" thinking.

Each chapter is substantially different in its emphasis and approach. The book critically examines the word "policy," explores some features of corporations associated with social policy, establishes a rudimentary understanding of markets, contextualizes poverty, provides a brief history of welfare and its reform, explores how disabled people are reluctant and inadequate participants in social policy, proposes modest modifications to Social Security, analyzes current health care policy, explores how private and public policy interpret children, suggests that a prevalent, if unspoken, category in private and public policy is that of "outsider," and suggests one way to confront the current assault on social policy. Of course, there are occasions for side trips, critiques, even ethical outrage.

In chapter 1, I attempt to demystify the word "policy," attaching it to the politics of people rather than viewing it as a commandment handed down by God, bureaucracy, or human nature. Usually policy is talked about as being public. It is more meaningful to explore both public and private policy and their interconnections. Because most policy is developed of, by, and for haves, a fact overlooked in much social policy writing, I find it important to draw a distinction at the start of the book between two classes, haves and have-nots.

The topic of chapter 2 is corporations, a far newer creation than society or polity. Corporations require public policy to work. Usually, private policy is corporate policy. Corporate policy is nondemocratic, in fact often anti-democratic, and often has a more important effect on people than much public policy does. Corporations may act with one another and with the public sector, workers, and consumers through markets. In this chapter, I suggest that the free market is a myth and that the modern market is in-creasingly controlled by corporations. Of particular interest is the new form the market has taken, and its attendant social, environmental, and political consequences, what has come to be called "globalization." Also discussed here and throughout this book are the profound consequences globalization has, perhaps unexpectedly, on social policy.

In chapter 3, I take an noncontroversial look at poverty and at wealth—and at a connection between poverty, wealth, and taxation. Some non-pecuniary dimensions to poverty are considered. Of necessity, the discussion is directed at the inequality between haves and have-nots.

Chapter 4 explores the remarkable creation called "welfare reform" and its consequences. An extraordinary phenomenon has occurred in the United States: welfare, rather than poverty, is considered the "problem"; that welfare and other transfer payments were attempted solutions to poverty and not the problem has apparently been forgotten. So-called welfare reform occurred in the context of an economy dominated by global corporations, a globali-zation that makes it difficult for any one country to maintain control over its economy.

The subject of chapter 5 is disability, which has become a nemesis to the welfare state and a challenge to social policy. Although one might imagine that the new digital, virtual, information economy would be better able to accommodate disabled people, the opposite is true. Because these aspects of our economy are significantly controlled by giant corporations, disabled people have become members of a larger group, outsiders, a subject taken up in chapter 9. When an able body becomes disabled, its fit with corporate organization becomes particularly problematic. Thus disabled bodies represent "able bodies" and their difficulties with contemporary corporate bureaucratic capitalism.

Social Security, the crown jewel of our social policy, is explored in chapter 6. The United States is "graying," yet not so much as other developed countries such as Japan. Aided by the media and the corporate requirements of a global economy, the increasing proportion of old people has become an unnecessary critique of Social Security, one that finds it bankrupt and only typical of the public sector's corruption of social policy. Like other forms of social policy, Social Security, one is told, is best left to the private sector. Perhaps nowhere is the assault on social policy as clear as in the attacks on Social Security. And nowhere are the issues so befogged by the media, government, corporate propaganda, transnational corporations, and the particular form that increasing globalization is taking.

Chapter 7 offers a reasonably straightforward account of our health care system, its deficiencies, and what needs to be done. Many people involved in health care policy essentially agree with the thrust of this chapter. Yet, the real world, or at least the one we are told is real, finds the solutions proposed for our health care system at best difficult, even utopian. In this chapter, one is called on to question a world that so imperils decency and common sense.

If the chapter on health requires only common sense, chapter 8, on children, demands more. We do not seem to understand children—the more you give them, the more they seem to want—yet we seem clearly to understand that children are resources for the future, their labor is to be cultivated as a commodity, their education aimed at increasing their human capital, that they are malleable and can be turned into assets for corporate society. Occasionally something goes wrong, and the world is disturbed by the clamor surrounding Elián González, by the prison sentence of Nathaniel Brazill, by the tragedy at Columbine.

Many aspects of the welfare state, indeed of social policy, are constructed, deconstructed, and then reconstructed by custom, bureaucracy, politics, and power. Samples of such categories, what I term "outsiders," are portrayed in chapter 9; these include mental illness, drug abuse and its treatment, and imprisonment. They issue from our social policy and are more connected to it, and to one another, than is apparent. There is a certain fungibility to these categories. In the future, one can expect that more mentally ill people will be "treated" by the criminal justice system, as, in the past, many mentally and physically disabled people were "helped" by institutions before the advent of "deinstitutionalization." As I suggest, these categories and others are connected to a global, corporate capitalism.

Books such as this one are often set aside, either gladly or reluctantly, with the ultimate comment: "This is all very nice, but what can we do to change things?" In the final chapter, I offer an answer to this question, given the rising tide confronting us in the new millennium, with most of us not even in boats but afoot, a tide in which only a few haves, if that, will be dry and most of us will be soaked. We should prepare for change, more rather than less, quickly rather than slowly. The social policy of the last century is under assault. It is my hope that the following pages will contribute to a better navigation of the current storm raging against social policy.

# 1   Policy

To define "policy" at the outset of an inquiry into its use is to perpetrate an injustice. Readers may come away thinking that they understand policy, can designate it like a specimen in a museum, may even have the illusion that being able to do so somehow constitutes knowledge. In fact, however, establishing the meaning of words is surprisingly difficult. In Western philosophy Plato first undertook the task, and subsequent philosophers have often been concerned with language and meaning. One possible understanding of policy might be that it is a socially constructed, authoritative, systematic set of rules that governs the allocation of resources. We could go on and list competing definitions of policy; we could modify our definition in their light. In the end, though, what would we have achieved? Would we have given readers insight? And what about defining such words as "authoritative," "rules," "governs," and "resources"? These are surely as troublesome as the term "policy." As is often the case, breaking one word into many, particularly if the constituents are more problematic than the initial word, explains nothing.

The plan in this volume is to alternate between presenting an ostensive definition of policy, in which the term is defined by offering examples that together provide a meaningful conception of it, and tracing the logic of its meaning. Thus certain social policies are examined and discussed within context.

Another preliminary clarification is needed. The word "social" is rarely used except as a modifier of the word "policy." Social policy is a subset of policy. Further, the word "society" is also avoided, except when its meaning is clear and uncontested. The term "society" is often as misleading as the word "America" (as in "What is good for society?" or "What is good for America?"). It is even more mysterious that society and America are spoken of as personal actors, even as benign clones of Orwell's Big Brother. Thus society needs, wants, or asks for more health; America declares a war on drugs; society needs better education; and society enters the revolutionary age of the Internet.

Only persons or organizations may want, or not want, something. As I shall argue explicitly, what "society" wants, needs, or asks for is usually what haves want, need, or ask for. Rarely are the needs and rights of have-nots discussed in the media, except as human-interest stories. Instead, have-nots are seen as objects of charity, as marginal people whom haves, in various fashions, wish to keep marginal. In short, society does not speak with one voice nor is it the human body writ large. In fact, the meanings of terms like "society," "America," "policy," "social policy," and "haves" and "have-nots" are contested and political, which will shortly become evident in this chapter and more broadly in this book.

The examples of social policy presented in this book contribute to an ostensive definition of policy. Significantly, and inevitably, they deal with private policy as well as not-for-profit and public policy. Evident throughout is that private policy is overwhelmingly corporate policy. Each example of social policy is presented differently so as to show the multitudinous facets of social policy. Accordingly, different perspectives will include political conflict, historical development, public discussion, the relationship of social policy to the welfare state, and the relation of both to private policy. Since much social policy redeems failures of the economy, pays for public support by taxation, and is now ostensibly moving from the public to the private sector, there is occasion for economic argument in the discussion of social policy (see chapter 2).

Seeking clarity, let us begin with examples of what policy is *not*. First, policy is not inherently ethical. The policies of Nazi Germany or Stalinist Russia are sufficient examples of this. Policy is also not neutral. Almost always, policy benefits some at the expense of others. It is also not God-given or natural, but is constructed by human beings. Only rarely is social policy fashioned as the answer to a social problem. Seldom, too, is a social problem discovered by experts. To expand our definition, let us examine the constituents of policy such as resources. These include material resources like money, goods and services, and time, as well as less tangible elements such as health, knowledge, beauty, skill, and so forth. Of course, explanations of additional resources such as life, liberty, and happiness would require volumes.

Words like "authority" and "govern" also require elaboration.[1] Authority might mean the legitimate use of power, but then what do we mean by legitimate?[2] Surely a parent's use of power to prevent a child from running into traffic is legitimate. The urgency of the situation and the parent's greater wisdom make it so. But it is a mistake to regard society as a family and to rely on the wisdom of the ruler, the ruling class, political parties, and so on. Further claims of legitimacy have enormous consequences and are properly open to question.

"Power" is a term central to politics and to political science. According to some, power is transitive, whereas others believe it is delegated.[3] Power exists both inside and outside government. Although many are uncomfortable with power, regarding it as a means of coercion, violence, and force, others are perfectly at ease with it, viewing it as a tool for freedom and autonomy. The word "power" is part of the Greek word for democracy, which, in Greek, means roughly "people's power or rule."[4] Almost all modern governments call themselves democracies, even though power may be concentrated, coercive, and violent. Most political scientists regard democracy in its literal sense as an ideal, at best, but more commonly as an illusion. The self-proclaimed founder of policy sciences, Herbert Lasswell, explicitly differentiated between the elite and the masses, reserving political action to the powerful and the influential. Variants of this view pervade modern political science.

Political science includes the ways that policies are made, implemented, and evaluated.[5] The most immediate revelation from political science is that policy is far more complicated, indeed messy, than is revealed in many texts on the subject. Another contribution from political science is more profound: *policy is the precipitate of politics*. Though not epiphenomenal, policy cannot be understood without understanding politics. And politics cannot be understood without comprehending power.

Power has been variously understood as a resource or a relationship. Viewed as a relationship, it is transitive, meaning that if A has power over B and B has power over C, then A has power over C.[6] As a resource, power can often be exchanged for other resources or values such as wealth, skill, and knowledge.[7] Power need not be confined to the political arena. It also exists in corporations, bureaucracies, and families. Indeed, recent formulations of power place it everywhere; manifest power is the coagulation of instances in which power may not be recognizable as such, as in categorizing, knowing, seeing, and labeling. Power is involved not only in categorizing, labeling, and knowing, but even in deciding where power does and does not exist. Although some conceptual danger is attached to thinking of power in such broad terms, it has become useful, perhaps even necessary, in today's world where power is often elusive, obscure, dispersed, and ubiquitous.[8]

Usually power and wealth are connected—wealth frequently buys power, and power often commands wealth. The powerful and the wealthy are linked to each other; indeed, they are frequently the same. Policy is a product of power, and since haves have more power than have-nots, it is not surprising that policy is so often made of, by, and for haves: people and organizations wielding power and wealth.

Politics and the policy that issues from it is usually contested. To the degree that the opponents are haves and have-nots, the contest almost always goes in favor of the more powerful haves. If the contestants are have-nots, formal policy is less likely to evolve, since the policy choices of contests between have-nots seldom have any bearing on the lives of haves. When it does (e.g., when drugs infiltrate suburbia, when crime harms haves, when deficient education makes too many have-nots unproductive), then haves may institute policy.

When those contesting the policy are haves, the policy in question may be war, truce, negotiation, or law. Minus the amendments, our Constitution is largely a compilation of agreements among haves. Of course, haves may occasionally downplay their differences to keep power from have-nots. All this must strike the person of principle as disagreeable, counterintuitive, even subversive. Nonetheless, most of it is there for the reading in those documents of, by, and for haves, including agreements governing commerce, corporations, bureaucracies, and so on, and may be readily glimpsed as well in the business press.

A disturbing aspect of the current use of power is that it is not the only conceivable use of power, although its public relations, when not obscuring the issue, would make us think it is. In fact, other uses of power are surely possible, such as power for democracy—power of, by, and for the people, including the have-nots, power to liberate and to do good.

Although haves may conspire against one another regarding policy, only rarely is the policy of haves over have-nots conspiratorial in nature among haves. Indeed, it is usually openly talked about for logical reasons: haves keep other haves informed since a free market of ideas is an advantage to them, particularly considering that largely haves buy and sell. It is worth noting that, as a rule, conspiracy theories are more misleading than what they are supposed to uncover. The difficulty lies in extracting the main events from the side shows that dominate the media.

Indeed, the media has become so significant that it is necessary to understand how elites make use of the media.[9] Important to this understanding is that the media are overwhelmingly owned by corporations. Like any business, their principle goal is profit, which may come from selling advertising space to other corporations. What appears on television as the evening news is only the tip of a gigantic iceberg that includes production, sales, and organization. The major networks are wholly owned by giant corporations. People engaged in the media are likely to live out most of their lives among haves.

Sex and violence sell not only in the movies but also on television, in magazines, and over the Internet, and thus dominate the news. The more than $40 million spent by the Office of the Independent Counsel on the Clinton scandals was dwarfed by the costs for and profits from covering the story. This was a story of importance, one routinely ignored by those who profess a distance from and boredom with the coverage of scandals and the differential coverage by various media shows on television, ranging from *Hard Copy* to *The NewsHour with Jim Lehrer*.[10]

During the cold war, there was not only an arms race but a propaganda race. The question was phrased crisply in the media, in education, and in public relations: Why is a country that is able to sell all sorts of goods and services losing the propaganda race with the Soviet Union? Whether we were indeed losing the race was at best questionable and was ultimately found to be untrue with the breakup of the Soviet bloc, which was attributed, in measure, to the permeation of new information technologies into the Soviet Union.

Both the Soviet Union and the United States took propaganda seriously. It not only played a role in the contest between haves in the Eastern and Western blocs but also was a factor in haves winning over the hearts and minds of have-nots in both blocs. Here the United States was ahead, since the use of crude forms of power, such as torture and murder, are less practiced on American citizens; in fact, haves' control over the hearts and minds of the have-nots reached such a high level in this country that violence was usually unnecessary. Of course, cruder forms of power did exist in the United

States in ghettos, prisons, and institutions comparable to the relation between haves and have-nots in some other countries. Although not usually conspiratorial, such exercises of brute force rarely made it into the media, have-nots generally not being the subject of saleable stories but rather marginalized, segregated, and kept apart from haves.[11] Although far from being true, equality of opportunity is a professed American goal. Equality of opportunity means upward mobility, which accounts for some of the popularity of the success and deeds of haves.[12]

Propaganda techniques, including public relations, advertising, and marketing, are openly taught at institutions of higher learning and widely practiced by the media, the government, and corporations. In such propaganda, morsels of truth exist—sometimes because of the necessity of communication among elites, sometimes as interesting stories tucked away, say, on page A-8, and sometimes where the media attacks elite interests to enhance profit.

Myths of extreme importance are routinely subjects of public relations. One such myth, which I discuss later, has to do with what is and what is not considered politics. Another, about the naturalness of free markets and private property, has had a reincarnation not only nationally but also globally. According to this myth, the Soviet bloc imploded because of the self-evident inefficiencies of state planning and the lack of privatization. There is some truth to this, but it is not the whole truth. According to the free market and private property myth, the once flourishing Asian tigers, which were taking advantage of U.S. free markets through Oriental wile, martial arts, industrial espionage, even a work ethic characteristic of the golden days of American capitalism (which we were striving to recover), in 1997 and 1998 were, in the midst of their economic crisis, revealing the bankruptcy of their other methods of gaining economic power. In fact, many American economists agree that there are indeed many ways toward achieving development,[13] a conviction the United States put into effect in its trade relations with China, ignoring such issues as human rights, prison labor, even national security.

The private free market fiction is an important achievement of the American media, the educational system, social discourse, and politics in an environment where corporations wield the power that they do. Examples of this myth include our recently booming Goldilocks economy, justifications for dismantling the welfare state, the entrenchment of newspeak,[14] such as flexible labor markets (meaning workers who are easy to boss around), special interests (meaning labor unions and environmental groups), jobs (meaning profits), globalization (meaning the ascendancy of transnational corporations over nation-states), welfare reform (meaning welfare repeal), privatization of Social Security (meaning increased corporate profit and destruction of the social safety net), and so on.

In fact, neither private property nor the free market is natural.[15] Both are social and political constructs relying on law, regulation, custom, even the threat of force. A market economy requires the legal structure of contracts, laws enforced against theft and bribery, other modifications to the market, and an effective system of taxation. This has become exquisitely clear as markets and private property overwhelm the former Soviet bloc. Indeed, the U.S. Constitution is substantially a set of regulations that govern markets. That the market requires laws and power for its operation and sustenance is clear. That these laws are natural, like, for example, the laws in Newtonian physics, has been claimed by some (e.g., the Austrian school of economists).[16]

Consider the family. Babies are not made to toil to earn their milk. Mothers give it to them even at the expense of a night's sleep. This is no market exchange. Should the father be a male chauvinist who uses his power over his wife to command obedience, this is also no market exchange. In fact, few relationships within the family are market exchanges. Rather, they involve love, altruism, obedience, and power. We know surprisingly little about human nature, but human nature may well account for more of what goes on in the family than markets, which may even be at odds with human nature. Karl Polanyi makes such an observation in his masterpiece, *The Great Transformation*.[17] Describing the transition from mercantilism to market capitalism, he dwells on the extreme social, personal, political, and legal changes that extend to the reconstruction of land, labor, and capital as commodities, which they had not been before. Market capitalism is a construction, not some natural law.

Although corporations may interact with one another and with consumers through markets, their internal workings may be bureaucratic, authoritarian, hierarchical, and nonmarket. Consider a stereotypical hunter-gatherer tribe. Here food is gathered and distributed to others, perhaps more according to their needs than to what they have to offer in exchange in a nonexistent market. Or consider this tribe at war with a neighboring tribe. Goods, booty, even lives may be taken by violence ungoverned by the rules necessary for a market. (Of course, wars exist today in flagrant violation of the rules governing markets.)

The conception of the market as a natural entity is a myth, but one that is of central concern to the media, propaganda, public relations, advertising, and corporations. Violation of market rules by have-nots are stigmatized as welfare, theft, and rudeness. When markets are violated by corporations, however, a different language is used: jobs are *protected*; legislation creates a *favorable* business environment; businesses form strategic *alliances* and have patent *agreements*. In general, it is only haves, the corporations, and stronger nations who are allowed to engage in extra-market transactions without stigmatization and marginalization including, but not restricted to, incarceration.

Markets are not inherently evil. Under suitable restrictions and democratic control, they provide for the economically efficient allocation of goods and resources, capital and labor, savings and investment. Although the choice between brands is often a parody of freedom, the supermarket is certainly preferable to rations. Market transactions between people of roughly comparable power enhance the well-being of participants. Indeed, far more could be said in praise of markets.[18] In the end, though, markets are good insofar as they serve people, although one sometimes hears that people are good insofar as they serve markets.

In large measure, politics and the social policy issuing from it are devoted to the care and feeding of markets. Given the centrality of markets to our lives and to the interests of corporations, this is to be expected. And, given power differences, it is also expected that politics and policy favor haves. Often there is no public argument. Even when there is, politics and policy are likely to follow the interests of haves, whose interests in social policy are likely to differ from those of have-nots.

The modern welfare state is incomprehensible without industrialism and market economies. In significant measure, the modern welfare state is best understood as making good on the market failures all economists recognize, such as externalities (e.g., unemployment insurance), imperfect competition (e.g., regulation), information costs (e.g., the Food and Drug Administration), and public goods (e.g., roads). (Of course, the examples given in parentheses are only pieces of an elaborate mosaic.) The modern welfare state also takes care of those situations where unfettered markets are simply too painful for too many people. Thus programs exist for disabled people, the poor, old people, children, and the unemployed. The distinction, central to a modern welfare state, between worthy poor and unworthy poor must be made in a uniform and bureaucratic manner.

A further logic for the existence of the modern welfare state in modern market economies was made possible by the British economist John Maynard Keynes, who fashioned a role for government in markets in ways transcending those Polanyi described. Before Keynes, it was thought that market economies could be at equilibrium only at high levels of production and employment. Keynes showed the contrary to be so, and advocated government intervention even in times of equilibrium at low levels of production and employment, such as in the Great Depression.[19] This new role of government led to an increased role of government in all sorts of programs, many extending beyond the necessity of the Keynesian mandate.[20]

In short, Keynes saved market capitalism by removing barriers between the government and the economy. During World War II, government intervention took the form of vast military expenditures that continued into the cold war and into today's economy. No longer were benefits for the poor seen as pernicious charity eroding the work ethic. Even if such effects existed, they could be rationalized in the name of the greater economic well-being.

Although inevitably connected to other policies, the social policies discussed in this volume largely issue from the politics and policies surrounding the labor market. The modern welfare state complements the modern market economy by making up for market failure, particularly in the labor market. Further, it takes care of people when and where the market cannot and makes up for excessive pain caused by the market. The word "excessive" is not in the eyes of the beholder, nor is it typically in the eyes of have-nots; rather, it is usually in the eyes of haves who make policy. Those welfare benefits (e.g., Social Security, unemployment insurance, Headstart, the WIC [Women and Infant Care] program, welfare as we knew it), bestowed in the face of excessive pain, can be withdrawn when that pain diminishes or when the term "excessive" is reinterpreted by haves. As haves may point out, such benefits are not rights but privileges.[21] But, contrary to that opinion, have-nots may still interpret them as rights, may even claim that such benefits are necessary.[22]

The policy and language of haves disguise many of the problems of have-nots. For example, consider homelessness. Whereas statistics consistently indicate a high incidence of homelessness among women and young children, the media (i.e., haves) continue to depict the "typical homeless person"

ale, insane, and drug addicted. Since policy and politics are so predi-
d on power, the word "empowerment" merits particular scrutiny. It is a
word that has become fashionable in the language of helping. However,
haves rarely exhibit an interest in empowering have-nots except on those
occasions when haves equip have-nots in a contest against other have-nots,
as typically happens in wars. Here, have-nots are empowered to conquer
enemy have-nots. Of course, in such cases, empowerment occurs in a strict
military hierarchy, where mutiny is a despicable offense. Have-nots are also
empowered by the apparatus of modern production. Have-nots may operate
expensive machines in the pursuit of making profits for haves. Typically the
armed forces and industrial corporations are characterized by powerful
mechanisms of control and are recognized as nondemocratic. Both corporations and the armed forces may verge on authoritarianism or even totalitarianism, an outcome to be expected from empowering have-nots in hierarchical, disciplined structures, where empowered have-nots are controlled
by haves.

Outside the context of such antidemocratic organizations, empowerment
is an illusion. As Frederick Douglass observed, power is never given freely
by the powerful but is won only as a result of the struggle of the powerless.
For example, in human services, empowerment is sometimes conceived as
making have-nots aware of their choices, such awareness supposedly constituting empowerment. The range of choices, however, is far narrower than
it is for haves. In truth, "empowerment" ensures that have-nots will abide by
the policies of haves and distorts power into the knowledge of a limited
number of choices. There is little reason for haves to empower have-nots,
but they have much to gain by giving have-nots a *sense* of power that, in
reality, the latter do not have.

Lapses in democracy are held just for the ultimate good of the state.
However, this does not change the power over firms, the armed forces, or
other organizations in which have-nots are empowered. Further, there is a
danger that lessons learned on the job, in the army, and so on may come to
permeate a person's life, or society as a whole, in public civic culture. As
for the increasingly corporate nature of society, workers regularly criticize
corporate abuse of power, although their criticism is most often directed at
their individual bosses, obviously the most visible incarnations of domination. Within such clearly antidemocratic organizations, newspeak has become popular, whereby war is defense and privatization represents large
corporations.

This is a natural consequence, one to be expected, from relations that are asymmetric in power. It characterizes politics, which ineluctably involves power. And policy is the harvest of politics. Understanding power is necessary in order to understand politics and policy. Power, of course, is present in innumerable places such as complex organizations and bureaucracies, even in the family structure. Power is often intrinsic to seemingly "objective" operations like categorizing, labeling, and quantifying. Reinterpreted by Michel Foucault, Sir Francis Bacon's dictum that knowledge is power has acquired new meaning.[23]

A decisive change in power has been its transformation by numerous technologies and disciplines into a force once thought impossible. Although power may be deployed in seemingly invisible ways, such power often intensifies and becomes highly visible.[24] While our main concern here is how power is applied to people, the growing application and refinement of power over the nonhuman environment cannot be overlooked. Today we have the power to protect ourselves from unreasonable heat and cold, to grow food in what once were deserts, to extend life, and, in general, to "control" our environment. Sometimes the exercise of power, however, has noxious side effects like pollution, environmental degradation, and the greenhouse effect.

An overwhelmingly important mechanism of power is the media's command of power. Occasionally technologies hide power, and sometimes they use power to achieve malignant ends but make it appear that their aims are benign. Our level of technology increasingly affects the media, public relations, and advertising, and becomes ever more expensive, more sophisticated, and more profitable.[25]

If policy issues from politics, and politics depends on power, then power is becoming ever more integral to corporations — not only in their internal structure but in their relations to people outside the corporation. The power of haves over have-nots is growing. Yet the preponderance of have-nots over haves sometimes enables them to exercise power — for example, during the Great Depression, the civil rights movement, and certain trade union activities.

Only rarely do the media, public education, even polite conversation mention power and, even then, usually in ways not directly connected to domestic politics. For example, the United States is a superpower; the names of the Dallas Cowboys, Denver Broncos, and other athletic teams connote power. Criminals may be portrayed as violent, and violence is an extreme manifestation of power, although the power of the criminal is usually exercised spasmodically, without political effect, indeed usually against have-nots. A media powerful enough to construct physical beauty, family values, the desirability of buying more and more stuff, and so on does not often portray or discuss power's connection to haves.

Another fallacy regarding politics is that it exists within a well-demarcated and limited range of political participation. The caricature of political participation is that it occurs during elections and is confined to voting for either a Republican or a Democrat. Indeed, the virtues of a society where people can choose between two candidates are converted into a civic duty. That fewer than half the voters vote is held a disgrace to our country, and one that is much discussed. Not voting means not doing one's part. However, to the extent that there is no difference between the candidates, not voting may be rational. In media portrayals of nonvoters, similar to the depiction of have-nots, those who do not vote are viewed as crazy, lazy, uninformed, indifferent, undereducated, unpatriotic, even criminal. Those who are better educated are exposed to an expanded notion of political participation: the need to communicate with, influence, and lobby one's elected representatives. Because elected representatives indeed pay attention to such activities, again the advantage falls to haves, as they control more money and have more direct contact with, access to, and influence on elected representatives.

We are told in high school that anyone can become an elected representative, even, and especially, president; of course, growing up in a log cabin and being truthful about cutting down cherry trees can only be advantages. This, of course, is a parody of the lessons we learn about equal opportunity for all. Only one person may be elected president. The number of political offices, of course, pale in comparison with the number of people in our country. This resembles the myth that professional athletics can more than rarely rescue one from poverty. In both cases, the extent to which money and other advantages come into play is ignored, privileges available to haves. In elections where individuals can make a difference, like voting for members of the local school board, few vote; for the most part, no one even expects it. Political scientists recognize that in a two-party system both candidates, confident of their base of support, usually move closer together on the issues during the campaign,[26] often making the vote of less consequence.

Another element of the political myth is the assumption that those in public office are the only fabricators of policy. This is blatantly untrue in a society where corporations and private policy dominate. Moreover, simply because an individual was once a have-not does not mean we should expect that person, on reaching high office, to represent the interests of have-nots. To be elected to high office in our political system requires the assistance and support of haves. President Franklin D. Roosevelt, in his efforts to help have-nots, has been called a traitor to his class. But rarely have Richard Nixon and Bill Clinton been accused of such treachery, although both are equally plausible traitors to their have-not origins. Of course, there was a difference between presidential candidates George W. Bush and Al Gore. For example, Bush promised more conservative judicial appointments and a tax cut favoring the wealthy. Gore was more supportive of environmental concerns and, at times, made overtures to African-Americans and to trade unions. While real and significant, these differences were less significant than their agreements on trade, the importance of education, the significance of world engagement, and military superiority. And, to be sure, even the New Democrats are to the left of Compassionate Conservatives, but these differences pale in comparison with those between Hoover and Roosevelt, Dewey and Truman, Eisenhower and Stevenson, Goldwater and Johnson . . . in short, Republicans and Democrats as they had traditionally been. Further, the differences between Bush and Gore, and even traditional Republicans and Democrats, are dwarfed by their similarities.

Often we become aware of important issues only if we spend an inordinate amount of time seeking information and studying matters, time few of us have. If important issues affect our everyday lives, perhaps we make a greater effort. Ultimately, however, the prevailing myth that political scientists call political participation is flagrantly loaded to benefit those who are more fortunate. Few are educated in the realities of power. To many, power is an abstraction, viewed as a product to be sold, the legitimation of greed, and the accumulation of worldly goods.

Not only are we told that our political tools are truncated and channeled, but ultimately we are informed that significant change is beyond reasonable expectation. But politics is not restricted to the myths we are taught or to the image portrayed by the media. Opportunities for political action are plentiful. Indeed, as evidenced by the women's movement, even the personal is political. Opportunities for significant political action surround us. For example, if our children are not receiving an appropriate education, we can organize with other parents, teachers, and so on, and work together to improve the school. Such activity has greater political impact than one vote in a presidential election. By becoming involved in our children's schooling, we may find ourselves confronting broader political issues refracted through the school, such as inappropriate funding, inadequate teaching, or racism. Organizing with other people may give us more than a *sense* of power; it may well give us power itself. Similar opportunities are present in other areas of our life, such as our work and our neighborhood. All such action is political. Thus we must question the assumption that our political participation is confined to electoral politics. By doing so, we come to see that our conception of politics has been safely packaged by our education, the media, and our political culture. A narrow concept of political action among have-nots is to the benefit of haves, for it is they who appreciate that political participation extends well beyond the voting booth; indeed, it is the kind of politics they practice and is connected to social policy.

One's fundamental conception of politics is a critical divide that separates haves from have-nots and that helps make the former the more influential group. Add to that haves' greater power and money, as well as their control of the media, public relations, and bureaucracies, and clearly the imbalance in power falls decisively in favor of haves. The temptation to believe we can do nothing, to become skeptics or cynics, or, even worse, to use our power against other have-nots may be alluring. Though an easy out, this temptation is just another myth. Because we may know love, friendship, justice, and freedom in our personal lives while not finding them in our social lives does not mean we should readily assume that such virtues are infantile and un-civilized—in short, that they must be changed given the demands of the real world. In a decent world, such virtues should be possible. Have-nots should seek power by reasserting the traditional meaning of politics.

The fact is that haves need have-nots; primarily they need their work. There simply are not enough haves to take over the duties of have-nots. Thus we have labor strikes, or the threat of strikes, whereby have-nots band to-gether with the help of trade unions and other organizations in an attempt to force haves into making concessions, such as many of those found in the modern welfare state. Such concessions help to give have-nots a glimpse of power and wealth, and often are occasions around which have-nots can organize in meaningful ways.

Whether we believe that in the long run democracy, justice, and decency will prevail or that they are doomed does not discount that have-nots can participate in politics and in the formation of policy. What is needed for an intelligent politics of have-nots are work, dedicated thinking, action, and rationality. Hence, in the chapters that follow, social policy is examined in its various guises in both the public sector and the private sector, where it has come to be increasingly, and significantly, located. After exploring examples of social policy, as well as the origins and effects of power and politics, it is my hope that an expanded definition of policy shall emerge. Although the welfare state as we have come to know it is diminishing, reasonable and decent politics and social policy are not dead. But neither are they inevitable. Indeed, social policy is under assault. The control of so much social policy by corporations and the corpocracy is an assault on have-nots by haves. Unfortunately, social policy can no longer be relied on to be beneficial for have-nots. And thus it is my hope that what follows will help the less powerful advance constructive and democratic changes in social policy.

# 2  Corporations

Over the years, American corporations have increased considerably both in size and in the control and power they wield, and recently their growth has been ever more rapid. Private policy has overwhelmingly become corporate policy. Corporate influence over public policy has increased as the power of people to control our government has decreased. While we are more liberated from disease, from the weather, and from other natural disasters and constraints, we are increasingly bound by the domination of corporations. Modern giant corporations have decisively affected private, public, and not-for-profit social policy.

Corporate power extends across the globe. Corporations deploy vastly increased global power both directly and through their influence on public policies. What were once national markets have become global markets, and the new world order is increasingly becoming a global, capitalist, corporate order. Corporations have become transnational as well, and much international commerce occurs within these corporations. The World Trade Organization (WTO), the North American Free Trade Association (NAFTA), and the European Union (EU) are increasingly controlled by these transnational corporations, whose influence complements that of global economic powers such as Europe, Japan, and, of course, the United States, which also substantially controls the World Bank and the International Monetary Fund (IMF). These various organizations remain impenetrable, their governance a mystery. Global agreements go unnoted, yet they affect our purses, our spirits, even our civic society.

Usually corporations deal with one another and with consumers through markets that refract much of their power. Both domestic markets and global markets affect significant portions of social policy. Despite advancing technology, many people worldwide are poor, oppressed, undesired, prone to disease, wretched, and vulnerable. An understanding of corporations and markets, and of global economic reality and theory, is essential in assessing social policy, since social policy must be viewed in relation to them. Without an appreciation of markets, particularly labor markets, individuals are susceptible to the conventional wisdom regarding social policy.

The modern welfare state provides public goods, regulates the supply of workers (e.g., through public education, unemployment insurance, and social security), and generally tries to make up for the pain inflicted on people by a supposedly free labor market.

Imagine an island, perhaps a blissful tropical paradise in the South Seas, populated by just two people—say, Jack and Jill. Jill has just woven a beautiful flower necklace from the surrounding flora. Jack has just finished his afternoon snack of papaya and coconut milk. Full on only half the papaya and a clamshell full of coconut milk, he offers to exchange the other half of the papaya and the remaining coconut milk for the necklace. By now Jill is hungry and has thought of a new creation. So she agrees, and the exchange is made. Each is better off than before the exchange. We know this because were it not true, either Jack or Jill or both would have refused to participate in the exchange. In this classic free market, all parties are completely free to act in their own self-interest. Such an exchange is the basic relationship of the market.[1] The snack and necklace are examples of economic goods and services.

Now, in contrast to this imaginary society of two, contemplate one that has many more people and many scarce goods and services, which we shall term "commodities." Exchanges in a complex economy are difficult without using money as an intermediary. Thus money is accepted by all. Here we have the skeletal construction of a market economy. Everyone is in his or her best economic state. In this sense, the market economy is an efficient allocator of market commodities.[2] Further, ongoing exchanges ensure continual optimal happiness within the constraints of scarce resources. Unfortunately, however, this supposedly real world is as imaginary as our tropical island. For example, it does not account for differences in individual endowment, which, in reality, are far from equal. Sufficient inequality makes freedom an abstraction. Everyone, of course, is free to sleep under a bridge.

In some countries, a poor family is free to sell its daughter into slavery. We are all free to sell our labor to pay our debts and to support our families. Still, although not a paradise, the market is *economically* efficient. With certain stipulations, this efficiency can even be proven mathematically.[3]

But political, social, and legal practices are necessary for a market economy to work efficiently, even on Jack and Jill's tropical island. For example, Jill cannot bop Jack on the head and steal the snack, although she might be happier to have both the snack and the necklace. Should Jack not fancy the necklace Jill has just made, he still might exchange the remainder of his snack for the promise of a future necklace. In everyday society, such expectations lead to contracts, torts, laws, lawyers, courts . . . a whole apparatus concerned with the construction and enforcement of agreements. If Jack were indeed to exchange his leftovers for a future promise, this promise may well lead to futures markets. Should Jack or Jill wish to buy hurricane insurance, this desire, generalized to everyday society, might lead to the purchase of all sorts of insurances. Insurance companies might then invest their revenues, which might lead to investment banking, stock markets, bonds, and so on.

In addition to questions of rules, public goods, contracts, taxes, and secondary markets, there is the problem of by-products of production (externalities). For example, if Jack decides to get his coconuts by cutting down the trees, this might result in a lack of shade, which may then lead to skin cancer in an unknowing Jill, exemplifying, in this case, an extremely destructive by-product of Jack's coconut consumption.

Economic externalities may take the form of pollution, environmental degradation, and so on; public goods may include free education, libraries, public parks, prisons, and public health, and may contribute to alleviate such domains as poverty, welfare, disability, social security, health care, and so on. In short, some public goods may go into social policy. In some measure, the welfare state makes up for market imperfections insofar as these imperfections relate to present or future labor (newspeak for "human beings"). Thus although the free market is an *economically* efficient allocator of goods and services, it does not, nor cannot, exist without remedies for what economists call market failures, failures that must be repaired by laws, taxes, and government—indeed, the very apparatus that, we often are told, inhibits American initiative and unjustifiably hinders our freedom.

We have assumed that Jack and Jill, in their tropical paradise, each behave in order to maximize their individual utility. But had we injected a hint of romance, perhaps a second possibility might have crossed our minds, that Jack and Jill care not only about their own happiness but also about each other's. Surely, they will eventually get married, raise a family, and live happily ever after. But in fact there is no way to make a judgment between these two versions of human nature, about which we know little. It is even possible that Jack and Jill's economic problems are solved not with markets but simply in the ways that many ordinary families solve them—through some combination of love, altruism, self-interest, communication, and authority. Rarely is there a general discussion as to when, where, and how markets should or should not be applied. These matters are typically decided by power holders, or haves. Critical, however, is that such discussions occur often in open, democratic forums.

So we leave Jack and Jill as the sun sets on their tropical island paradise and return to the real world with the caveat that, most agree, economists' conceptions of this world are generally simplified. To modern market economies, which include people, commodities, money, services, government, laws, and contracts, we turn to another addition: corporations.

Most of us do not exist alone; rather, we live our lives interacting with other people. Our social experience is realized, in part, through complex organizations—for example, corporations—and they involve power. In their first incarnation, corporations were chartered by the state and enjoyed certain privileges that the state bestowed on them. A famous example of such a corporation was the East India Company, which was chartered by the British Crown. Its success was important to the state, and the risks it faced were many. Granted privileges by its state charter, like military protection, geographic monopoly, and mechanisms for pooling public and private resources, the East India Company was a brilliant success, at least for its British owners, the consequences for its workers being more questionable.

Other European countries chartered their own versions of corporations, and they proved to be a wonderful means of enhancing commerce between their native countries and other areas. Sometimes corporations from different countries expanded into the same area. A round of wars commenced, not so much from competition between the corporations as from that between the governments that chartered them. World War I is acknowledged to be an example of such a war.

Imperial wars—that is, wars between countries with competing claims to commercial dominance—do not exhaust the category of wars involving the United States, much less the rest of the world. Still, many wars are recognized as having resulted because of competing corporations under the protection of the motherland or fatherland. Armies and navies increased in both quantity and quality, a development greatly enhanced by the Industrial Revolution.

The U.S. Constitution ensured businesses that they would enjoy government protection. We expanded to the West, where we conquered the Indians; to the Southwest, where we defeated the Mexicans; and to the Southeast, where we bought out the French. We were large, and most of our commerce was internal since we were our own best customer. It was in the nineteenth century when the modern U.S. corporation took off. As in most wars, the Civil War in the United States shifted wealth and opportunity, in part from the vanquished to the victor. Further, not atypically, the Civil War also created new economic conditions within the victorious North. To varying degrees, these led to new industrial empires in steel (Carnegie), banking (Morgan), and oil (Rockefeller), as well as to the success of many other industries of lesser fame, bringing wealth to their founders, entrepreneurs, tycoons, and robber barons.

In order to grow, businesses required capital. Some was borrowed, but it was supplemented with the sale of shares and by borrowing on the value of the company as provided by the stock market. The greater the market valuation of stocks, the more money investors were willing to supply and the lower the interest rates. Further, corporations separated ownership from management.[4] Although some viewed this as democratic, it served to enhance the power of management. As industries expanded, they developed bureaucracies for management, domination, and control. In the United States, the important bureaucracies were in the private sector. Bureaucracies are a unique social form most eloquently examined by the sociologist Max Weber. This form is not restricted to government but also exists in corporations. Corporate bureaucracies figure prominently in this book.

The United States contributed greatly to the evolution of the corporation. Perhaps its greatest contribution has been the concept of limited liability, which allows corporations to raise capital by selling shares to investors who need not worry about their investment beyond the amount they invest. Unafraid of debt—or, worse, debtors' prison—investors were willing to buy shares of equity in enterprises not run by their families or close friends. Limited liability led to corporations in which management could be increasingly distant from owners. Limited liability did not arise out of market mechanisms, however. (For this reason, *The Economist* opposed it until 1925.) Limited liability required laws, an example of Karl Polanyi's more general observation that capitalism requires a culture that includes laws.

Some of us desire immortality. We hear talk of presidential legacies. One psychoanalyst described the Chinese Communist Party as Mao's attempt to ensure his revolutionary immortality.[5] Nineteenth-century tycoons not only desired immortality, but developed a means of approaching it, by organizing their businesses into bureaucratic corporations that would continue to operate after their death.[6] The government furthered the corporation by statute and by executive and judicial decisions. Perhaps the most startling example was the Supreme Court's judicial interpretation of the Fourteenth Amendment, originally intended to extend rights to former slaves, to ensure rights to corporations by considering them persons eligible to the rights granted by the Fourteenth Amendment.

Thus judicial decisions transformed the modern corporation into an entity with constitutional rights that people should enjoy. However, powerful corporations actually decreased individuals' rights in the private sector. Further, where corporations had once been chartered for a fixed period, now they were immortal. In their internal workings, bureaucratic corporations, through their business practices, largely replaced the market, although today such practices as outsourcing effectively cause modern corporations to work somewhat more through the market. In external relations, corporations became accustomed to their newly bestowed "citizenship" to augment their power over people and to influence governments.[7]

Taxes, essential to maintain programs of the welfare state, are often distorted in capitulation to corporate power. As the *Boston Globe* reported:

> The tax code offers a special benefit to companies that move jobs offshore, a gift also accepted by Massachusetts employers such as Stratus Computer Inc. of Marlborough (500 layoffs last year), Augat Inc. of Mansfield (260 layoffs) and the Shrewsbury division of the Quantum Corp. (85 layoffs), among others. It is one of many tax breaks that ripple perversely through the economy—favoring multinationals over

small firms, investors over average taxpayers and foreign workers over those at home.[8]

Although corporations may act through markets with consumers, workers who sell their labor, and other corporations, they are largely organized internally to conflict with democratic notions. Internal corporate authoritarianism is often neglected in political theory as well as by the media, public relations, propaganda, and corporations, where "private rights" is newspeak for "corporate rights."

Corporate monopolies and oligopolies give corporations significant control over markets in which they should only be participants. The government's awareness of this became apparent by interventions such as the Sherman and Clayton Antitrust Acts and the trust busting of the progressive era. Yet the struggle against trusts has still not been won and at best is ongoing. (In 2000 the government brought a significant antitrust case against the Microsoft Corporation.) Some have argued that trust busting has become less essential with globalization, because of the competition from other nations.[9] Resourceful corporations, however, have expanded transnationally, have made international mergers, and have developed multinational strategic alliances. The competition necessary for an efficient market is continually challenged. Corporations and the corporate sector have indeed become powerful, overwhelming the public sector.[10]

At the end of World War II, it was clear that Soviet power would be considerable, that European colonialism was no longer viable, that two largely European world wars should not be followed by a third, and that the United States, the dominant world power, was to fill Europe's power vacuum. New international organizations developed to deal with a bipolar world dominated by the United States, with the Soviet Union in second place. The United States retained its defense capability, helped reconstitute a devastated Western Europe through the Marshall Plan, and led the world in forming the United Nations and in establishing a new postwar economic system at the Bretton Woods Conference. Both the United States and Western Europe entered a period of prosperity, increasing corporate power and extending the welfare state in Western Europe and, to a lesser degree, in the United States.

The British delegation to the Bretton Woods Conference was headed by the eminent economist Sir John Maynard Keynes. Keynes had been a minor participant at the Versailles Peace Conference, whose outcome, he had predicted, would lead to World War II;[11] he wished to avoid similar mistakes at the end of World War II. The Bretton Woods Conference led to the General Agreement on Tariffs and Trade (GATT), the World Bank, and the International Monetary Fund. Because the United States was the most powerful nation, it is not surprising that both the World Bank and the IMF are located in Washington, D.C., and that all these institutions are controlled, to a considerable extent, by the United States.

Modern technology enables capital to move easily. This free flow of capital holds the economic policy of one country hostage to international markets, which became more speculative. Workers in the United States are threatened with the loss of their jobs to cheaper labor in other countries should they become too forceful about their wages and rights. International tax lawyers advise corporations as to which nations have the most favorable taxation, the fewest environmental burdens, and the lowest labor costs—in short, which nations offer the most opportunity for profit.

Today trillions of dollars circulate around the globe in capital markets, dwarfing the monies exchanged for goods. In 1997 the collapse of Thai currency led to problems with many Asian currencies and ultimately those of Russia and Brazil as well. Extensive loans were made but with conditions attached; borrowers were to maintain austerity and transparency, fit the mold of Western economies, wage an assault against social policy, and undertake other forms of restructuring. The free flow of capital is recognized as dangerous, as it can hold nations hostage to banks, to speculators, to hedge funds, and to corporations. The economist James Tobin, a Nobel laureate, has suggested that international monetary flows be taxed.

America was "discovered" and exploited partially in the search for gold to pay for spices made rare and expensive because of the cost and difficulty involved in the spice trade, in which, as it happens, the East India Company was engaged. Technological advances often break down the natural barriers to efficient free trade—for example, bigger ships, the Suez and Panama Canals, steam power, used not only for manufacturing but to provide energy for trains and ships, and so on.

Natural barriers to trade decreased, enhancing international trade. Early international trade involved such goods as spices, olive oil, and jewels. Later, less precious cargoes of cotton, rubber, oil, cloth, and automobiles depended on technological advances to overcome natural trade barriers. Technology, or so the myth goes, enabled mankind (the myth is male) to subjugate, conquer, dominate, even ravage nature, all in the name of progress.

Not all barriers to trade are natural. Pirates, for example, were a hindrance to overseas trade. Sir Francis Drake's attacks on Spanish shipping earned a knighthood from the Crown. Stagecoach and train robbers, and various violations by other offenders, augmented the technologies of policing, armed forces, and war. Other important barriers to free international trade include tariffs, import quotas, tax subsidies, industrial policy, and trade sanctions.[12]

Ostensibly we live in a brave new global world. But just as free domestic markets have never, nor will ever, operate without the influence of government and society, so it is with free global markets, which require laws, customs, treaties, contracts, and so forth to exist. Further, if we wish these markets to serve people rather than the other way around, additional modifications are only reasonable and just, such as taxation, regulations, provisions for those who cannot work, and numerous government social policies. National markets must mesh with the agreements, treaties, and international organizations that occur in a global economy; moreover, these markets and the international arrangements into which they enter must be governed democratically. Yet democratic governance and civic society have diminished in scope, while trade, markets, and capitalism have greatly increased in power.

With the collapse of the Soviet Empire, and with it the Eastern bloc, there was brief talk of a peace dividend from savings on anti-Soviet military expenses accruing to the United States in a world where it was now the sole superpower. German reunification gave a boost to the creation of a European Union and to the expansion of NATO. The effects on social policy in Europe and in the United States were profound, although not inevitable.

European integration has demanded a confluence of interest rates, corporate policy, free trade, and fiscal policy. Norbert Walter, chief economist of the Deutsche Bank Group, wrote with relief, in the *New York Times*, of the demise of European social policy:

> The German parliament is agreeing on sensible tax cuts . . . corporate taxes would fall even below the level in the United States. . . . The good news spreads well beyond Germany. Italy, too, is tackling pension reform. France is undergoing bruising mergers in the oil, banking and chemical industries. And, in a remarkable departure from past practice, French corporate executives have supported foreign ownership and influence in French stock markets. . . . Since the Reagan era, Americans have pushed Europe to embrace market reforms. At long last the message has been heard.[13]

European social policy has been ravaged by the lowering of social expenses, privatization, and corporate dominance. Indeed, corporate power is so influential in both private and government policy that what we may once have called "democracies" are often more accurately described now as "corpocracies." Economic integration depends on the standardization of macroeconomic policy. Although such standardization need not favor haves over have-nots, this is currently the case and influences EU participants.

Trimmed of fat, European corporations and welfare states are fast becoming as lean and mean as the corporations and welfare state in the United States. Welfare states in Europe have weakened, as has the welfare state in the United States. Under the tight supervision of the Federal Reserve, the United States enjoyed a prolonged period of slow growth. Corporate power has increased dramatically, accompanied by the expected effects on tax policy, trade policy, and labor policy. The slow pace of our economic growth since the Carter administration is not part of the average media account that trumpeted the Dow Jones average, technological (corporate) progress, the creation of jobs (most often those with the lowest salaries and the least benefits), and increased efficiency in the corporate sector.[14] Efficiency in health care, however, often translates into inferior health care for working people and have-nots because of managed-care programs and HMOs. Flexible labor markets translate into job insecurity and a willingness to work for less. Deregulated corporations mean more profitable, more powerful corporations. Perceived efficiency in welfare means less money paid out for welfare, fewer people on welfare, and the evolution and privatization of welfare programs. And, meanwhile, the interests of more and more powerful corporations become increasingly global.

In the corporate version, international markets amplify domestic injustices, such as increased differences between rich and poor, environmental degradation, and technologies of violence on a global scale. Examples from the past include British tariffs on Indian cotton goods, which devastated the nascent textile industry; U.S. barriers on petroleum goods, which contributed to Japan's attack on Pearl Harbor; U.S. steel quotas; and favorable tax treatment of influential U.S. corporations. This history was in no sense inevitable; it was more the product of national, corporate, even individual greed that operated only secondarily by breaking the rules but more typically by the powerful writing their own rules.

But people now are somewhat uneasy. We are entering the world of the Internet, and already our relation to knowledge and to one another has been transformed. Moreover, the Internet has empowered us—anyone can have his or her own Web page, and anyone can e-mail the president. We are a cultivated consumer society, yet many of us hate to shop. The gap between haves and have-nots has increased within countries worldwide, and this represents more than individual domestic issues; it is a global problem. Not only is the gap increasing between haves and have-nots within nations, but the rich and powerful developed countries are growing richer and more powerful while Third World countries fall farther behind.

Large corporations have also grown bigger and wealthier. Their power has increased as well, including their control over people, governments, and large national and international economic programs essential to social policy. It is apparent to most that corporate money sometimes can buy elections, but this is only one example of corporate power. Others abound. Corporate influence on legislation runs deep; politicians and corporate leaders are buddies; and our two-party system is rigged in favor of corporations, as little significant difference exists between the two parties. Further, corporations largely underwrite our not-for-profit sector. As one would expect, not-for-profit corporations rarely challenge corporate power. Corporate mergers in the United States in 1998 exceeded the value of those in any past year, and the resultant companies are larger and more powerful than ever.

The welfare state is funded by taxes. Powerful corporations, like average individuals, do not pay more taxes than is legally required. But unlike most people, corporations are assisted in filing tax returns by professional accountants, tax lawyers, and lobbying; indeed, corporations contribute to writing the law under which they are taxed. The United States spends a smaller proportion of its gross domestic product (GDP) on social policy than any other industrialized nation. On February 19, 2000, New York Times reporter David Cay Johnston published an article in the business section entitled "Corporate Taxes Fall, but Citizens Are Paying More," which helped in explaining the current state of social policy. Since 1990, the corporate tax burden has fallen dramatically, which one would expect given the corporation's increased power vis-à-vis the state. "Corporate tax shelters are our No. 1 problem" in enforcing the tax laws, stated then Treasury Secretary Lawrence H. Summers in an interview, "[and] not just because they cost money but because they breed disrespect for the tax system."

One symptom of the current mobility of capital and immobility of labor is that the income taxes corporations paid in 1999 dropped 2.5 percent from the previous year; at the same time, income taxes individuals paid rose by 6.2 percent, all this during an economic boom. At one time, corporations

had been concerned about promoting a public image a'
Today, however, tax departments in large corporations
are under increased pressure to enlarge profits with '

While tax departments and outside tax attorneys an.
handsomely rewarded by corporations that are aware of their u.
to the bottom line, the same does not hold for the Internal Revenue Sei.
which is underfunded by Congress. Not only is the IRS too understaffed to
perform sufficient corporate audits, but federal salaries do not begin to compete with corporate ones. Often, the IRS provides postgraduate training for
corporate tax attorneys in a revolving door familiar from other branches of
government. Further, the tax laws are too complex for most save corporate
tax experts. For example, often the legislation on tax shelters is drafted in-
correctly. All this provides a friendly playing field for the highly paid tax
professionals whom the rich and corporations can and do pay for.

Just as the natural free market is a myth, requiring substantial social and
political involvement simply to exist, so, too, is the notion of free international trade. The restrictions, agreements, treaties, customs, and so on necessary for free international trade can be written in a multitude of ways, some
hostile to the less powerful and poorer countries and to the poorer people in
countries that are thriving, others friendly, even nurturing, of the human
spirit. The most important international association governing international
trade is the World Trade Organization, in which, as in most cases, the strong
set the rules. Powerful corporations, often multinational, and their governments ensure that the international market will not be freer than necessary,
except insofar as market freedom benefits them. (Even half a century ago, the
United Fruit Company enlisted the State Department and the Central Intelligence Agency [CIA], run by the brothers Dulles—John Foster, secretary of
state, and Allen, CIA director—to overthrow Guatemala's democratically
elected government of Jacobo Arbenz Guzmán, which threatened to redis-
tribute land against the interests of United Fruit, now part of Del Monte.)

Labor movements have been pummeled by corporations. Natural resources have been plundered by trade. Gaps between the rich and the poor
have increased within countries, and between rich and poor countries. Indigenous populations have been ravaged. Child labor, abysmal working conditions, pitiful wages, and wage slavery exist in many Third World countries
and even in the United States. The ratio of wages to corporate profits in the
United States was never lower before the slide of the stock market than since
the days just before the Great Depression.

According to economic theory, everyone is better off under free trade, in the sense that gainers can compensate losers and still be better off. According to theory, free international trade brings with it an increasing gap between haves and have-nots within countries, although not as great a split as the one we currently see. But solutions to this are available, like better education and vocational retraining for workers whom free trade displaces, a more progressive tax structure, greater public investment in the future, and protection of indigenous peoples, who, like all others, have an inherent right to survival and self-determination. These individuals exemplify the need, for example, for enjoying alternative social arrangements, for having more resources invested in social policy, for protecting the environment, and so on. This is not what currently exists, however. Of course, it is understandable that powerful corporations use their power, that stronger nations seek to impose their will on weaker nations, that powerful corporations seek to save money and maximize profits, that nations dominated by tenacious corporate bureaucracies pursue mean and lean options in their internal conditions so as to overtake their global competitors.

Free global or regional market coalitions like NAFTA and the EU must come to agreements regarding standardization. But it is neither understandable nor forgivable that agreements toward commonality should necessarily entail a competition to drastically increase the difference between rich and poor and ignore democratic institutions and environmental protection. Giant corporations control not only their workers but the polity and civic society itself. Indeed, corporate domination is so extensive that only state power can control it. Unfortunately, the history of state power in the twentieth century has been loathsome, highlighted by Nazism and Stalinism. However, there is another form of civic power. Although democracy has been commonly subverted in the twentieth century, this book advocates a free state, where meaningful participation is possible, where public concerns are individual concerns, where power is not exercised by totalitarianism, militarism, Stalinism or fascism, but rather, as President Lincoln put it, of, by, and for the people, in short, meaningful authentic democracy, not "corpocracy." One version of democratic change is suggested in chapter 10.

The corporation in its modern form, with its increasing bureaucratic organization, precludes democracy, never mind other civic virtues such as freedom and meaningful participation. Indeed, corporations that advocate free-market capitalism, except when it imperils them, do not usually use markets to allocate goods internally. Business practices within corporations have always been largely bureaucratic. Markets, in fact, are not antagonistic to bureaucracies, as it is sometimes said, but rather function well together.[15] The modern bureaucratic corporation has become the private equivalent of public authoritarianism, domination, and the invasion of privacy.

Over the past twenty years, large modern corporations have increasingly downsized, outsourced, divested themselves of subsidiaries, and employed digital technologies and high-tech means of controlling inventory. They have emerged as the mean and lean corporations so dear to the hearts and pocketbooks of modern corporate America. In this latest phase, many corporations have merged; indeed, 1998 saw a peak in the market value of mergers. The reasons for these mergers were not solely to reduce costs, but often gave large corporations increased or oligopolistic power on the market. Further, modern corporations have also tended to outsource benefits and pensions to insurance companies and 401Ks, facilitating the hiring and firing of employees. Middle management becomes disposable. Chief executive officers (CEOs) work to increase the bottom line, to produce short-term increases in stock values, and to respond to shareholders' demands for short-term profits—their billowing salaries a product of their abilities to do this. Most important, the market has made substantial inroads in corporations, which now are more likely to buy legal and accounting services, factors of production, and so forth on the market. These changes eliminate unnecessary inertia from the modern restructured corporation, enabling it to take advantage of new markets and technologies. That the modern corporation makes frequent use of the market when it benefits by doing so, however, does not obviate the fact that most internal dealings of corporations are conducted not by means of the market but by business practices. Such practices, far from making corporations less powerful, have made them more influential in politics transnationally and, invigorated by digital technologies, ever more dominant. The power of the people, even of nation-states, has not kept pace.

Our jobs have changed; no longer are we secure in them or loyal to the corporations that employ us. Anger on the job is a newly researched issue. Jobs so structure the days that even when workers are off the job, they spend much of their time commuting to work, thinking about their job, talking about it to others. At home, workers may watch television simply to calm down, relax, distract themselves from thinking about their job. Since time-consuming chores occupy much of the modern worker's life, particularly if that worker is a homemaker and a parent—and some time must be reserved for sleep, of course, if only to prepare for the next day's work—a job has concrete implications for marriage, friendship, parenthood, and citizenship. While the modern corporation is solicitous of its employees' "input," its bureaucracy and domination render authentic participation irrelevant, make one's job the dominant element of one's life, and even at times keep workers awake at night or inhabits their dreams.

In 1997 the baht, Thailand's currency, was devalued, which affected not only the everyday lives of Thais but all of Asia. With the exception of the Pacific theater in World War II, the Korean War, and the Vietnam War, Asia's concern to most Americans has been inconsistent. (That Asia was of profound concern to some Americans, however, is evident by the very existence of these wars.) In any case, Americans, who had envied the miracle of Asian economic development, soon scorned the structure of Asia's economies, its societies, even its people. Two bulwarks contained what the U.S. media sometimes referred to as the "Asian contagion": namely, Japan, which has become profoundly tied to the West since World War II (before the war it was a major regional power), and China, which kept its currency pegged to the dollar at some internal cost. Had Japan and China not remained firm, the downward Asian spiral might have ended disastrously. As it was, the Asian economic crisis leap-frogged China and Japan to Russia and Brazil. It was no flight of fancy to have expected that the European and U.S. economies would also become imperiled. All this, of course, is history.

The lesson, however, is that, both for criticism and reform, it is insufficient to consider the United States as separate from other nations of the globe. That the United States is connected to other nations through treaties, the United Nations, tourism, and trade is obvious. Less apparent are the nature and extent of such connections, as well as other significant ties like increased multinational markets, the mobility of capital across national borders, legislation limiting immigration, and tax advantages that come with locating a firm in one country or another. All have profound effects on our internal markets and those of other countries, increase the differences between haves and have-nots, radically affect social stability, and influence what may already have become the ruination of the welfare state, never mind the havoc wrought on the less fortunate. Thus, in addition to politics, factors that depend on a global economy include a nation's power, bureaucracy, markets, corporations, social policy, and welfare state. How, where, when, and why this came about are not intuitively obvious. A volume about American social policy cannot fully examine what the famous but underrated philosopher Jeremy Bentham first called "international trade." But because international economics directly affects American social policy, some brief consideration of this subject is merited. Therefore, the following mentions some characteristics of international trade (many of them amplified by Dani Rodrik):[16]

- International trade, of course, is significant even to the United States, with its extensive internal markets and many natural resources.
- If for selfish interests alone, the United States must be concerned about the rest of the world. The expansion of market economies is far past the point where economic difficulties may be assumed to be self-contained.
- Global markets create severe, often new tensions with civic society, social values, social policy, and culture. In significant measure, these tensions are the result of a new asymmetry: whereas at one time workers could travel more easily than capital (e.g., immigrants seeking work would travel to factories forced to remain in their location because of transportation access, the availability of power, the proximity to inputs, and so on), now it is relatively easy for factories to relocate their operations to take advantage of cheap labor; investment capital is extremely mobile; and most workers cannot move to places where jobs are presumed to exist. Further, workers are willing to accept more substantial cuts in wages to avoid moving or losing their jobs. The results have been weaker labor movements, lower wages, less job security, and increasing differences between the interests of workers and capital, employees and corporations, and haves and have-nots. This pattern is true not only internationally but in the United States as well.
- International trade increases the tension between a particular nation's culture—including its norms, values, and institutions—and the uniform, bureaucratic practices of corporations that produce goods for export to other corporations in other countries or for transnational corporations. For example, economic development may adversely affect a nation's indigenous people.
- The dismantling of the welfare state is *not peculiar to the United States*; rather, it is an international artifact of global markets.
- Insofar as regions attempt greater economic integration—for example, in the EU and NAFTA—greater standardization is to be expected among participants, including, particularly in Europe,

standardization in social policy, interest rates, and national identity. (Young Europeans, particularly those who have power and money, increasingly identify with Europe as a whole rather than with their own particular nation. The phenomenon is not new; more than two hundred years ago thirteen U.S. colonies formed a Union with similar consequences. Indeed, viewing the United States as separate states that have become united is illuminating in thinking about globalization.)

- Indirect outcomes of international trade profoundly affecting developing countries derive from the elasticity of labor, which affects workers' bargaining power; the prevalence of wars, which occur disproportionately in these countries; and their relatively small and frequently unstable economies.

- Global trade optimizes economic efficiency (as does domestic trade). But international trade goes further by enabling each country to do what it does best (this comparative advantage is often forgotten in arguments against globalization). Unfortunately, differences between haves and have-nots increase in countries participating in international trade, which is a problem of internal distribution and redistribution. Thus questions of justice and fairness emerge anew with global trade. Economists underplay these matters; multinational corporations override them; and have-nots suffer. Such arguments are over not only workers' salaries, but also child labor, environmental degradation, social disintegration, and political dictatorship.

- In practice, international trade makes capital less vulnerable to taxation since capital has generally become so mobile. Thus the policies and programs of welfare states funded by taxes decrease at the same time that they become more essential, since it is difficult to tax movable capital but easy to tax relatively immobile labor. Capital, in bargaining with labor, passes the costs of "fringe" benefits onto labor (in our country, what rapidly springs to mind is the destruction of welfare, the impending restructuring of Social Security, Medicare, and Medicaid, and the increasing privatization of the public sector).

Elicited in the list are some economic justifications for markets. Although incomplete in number and detail, these arguments cannot be brushed aside (although there is room for further discussion). In short, in themselves markets are economically efficient, enhancing the globe's economic state to where everyone would be better off if the winners compensated the losers. The welfare state might plausibly be regarded as such compensation, haves compensating have-nots for the sake of social stability, altruism, and the like. However, as this country enters the new global economy, such compensation may seem a less warranted or needed expense.

The issues cited earlier are theoretical consequences of free trade, sufficient in themselves to dismiss the arguments of Ross Perot, Pat Buchanan, and other isolationists. However, the realities of a political economy are not necessarily in accord with the words and equations of economic theory. Thus, in practice, poor people and poor countries are unlikely to have the power necessary to affect the decisions of the rich, whether individuals, corporations, or countries. For example, affluent countries, particularly the United States, set the agenda for negotiating treaties in global trade. Poor countries are unlikely to have the resources to hire experts to represent them in disputes. And, further, powerful countries like the United States are likely to override the provisions of treaties that go against their national security interests. In short, powerful countries structure the wording of treaties, have undue influence in their implementation, and often include escape clauses. Nothing similar may be said of poor countries, which might be further constrained by shackling debt to the IMF or the World Bank and by other critical needs that emerge in their multitudinous and complex relations with rich nations.

Further, there are restrictions on the market that decency demands. Vital organs are still not allowed to be sold. Nor are children sold to childless couples, medical researchers, or child molesters. Keeping certain items off the market is entirely common and at times may exemplify a conflict between markets and decency. What one should consider an economic good subject to market principles is a vital topic for political discourse. Only such discourse keeps the market legitimate. Of course, corporate or political elites may prevent or dominate the discussion. Such interference is fair only to the extent that might makes right. Since this is not our belief, any political discourse ought to be democratic. Such discourse considers the virtues of markets, yet also realizes that markets are artificial tools designed to serve people, not to dominate them. Hence the proper role of markets is both an appropriate and a necessary topic in democratic political discourse and policy discussion. Those organizations with power to regulate global markets such as the WTO, IMF, and World Bank are substantially mysterious, their governance unknown.

Thus far I have outlined some consequences of economic theory as they apply to the global economy when it is working more or less properly. Some of these effects are straightforward expansions of standard economic theory as applied to the globe; some have been verified by empirical econometric work; and all must be considered in any proposed change to that system, including democratic change. The current global market system is vulnerable to even modest shake-ups such as the devaluation of the Thai baht, not to mention significant events like war, the depletion of natural resources, environmental degradation, and pollution.

It bears repeating that the global market system (and national markets) are neither natural, God-given, nor otherwise engraved in stone. Rather, markets, both national and international, are steeped in history, culture, and customs. Markets work because of civic assurances, as well as laws, guaranteeing that rules are followed accompanied by appropriate mechanisms of enforcement. International markets are even more tenuous than national markets, for usually international courts and other such forums are weaker than their national counterparts and unable to rule uniformly on disputes. (Recently, however, people who believe that the rights of others are being denied are bringing organizations and transnational corporations to democratic discussion. Such considerations, although signaling that markets do not stand alone, are often forgotten, and important questions such as whether global markets should exist, and, if so, where, when, and how, are not often directly addressed.)

The current consensus is that free markets in our society and across the globe should exist, although they are far from perfect. They are efficient systems of economic distribution and competent allocators of economic resources. But markets are only one element of civic society and must be held accountable to it. They are made to serve people and not the other way around. Acts that are unacceptable to a decent society may either violate or be consistent with markets. In either event, they are reprehensible. Whether an act interferes with the market is of only secondary concern to a decent society whose central considerations are democracy, freedom, efficiency, settling disputes without resorting to violence (Hobbes's criterion),[17] equity, the reduction of unnecessary pain, and democratic control of labor, land, and capital. It is by such criteria that private, not-for-profit, and public policies should be measured, and this is how such policies encountered in the following pages should be considered.

Market criteria have a place. We do not wish resources squandered, capital misdirected, or labor abused. The market can be a valuable mechanism, certainly in the short term, but it should not be totally unrestrained. However, markets are used by corporations to control resources, labor, and, increasingly, the nations of the globe. Modern corporations have grown to the extent that some have the power not only to control their workers but to influence policies affecting corporate interests and to sway the behavior of national governments. Corporations effect transnational mergers, sending their capital to enterprises where returns are the greatest, increasingly in other nations.

The influence corporations wield over other nations, as well as our own, affords them the power to affect public policy, even to the point of war. Their influence in our country has grown because of their enormous expansion in size, the greater mobility of capital, and international expansion, which includes mergers with foreign corporations as well as the presence of foreign corporations in the United States. The disintegration of the Soviet bloc has brought us closer to becoming a global market, which may indeed be viewed as an improvement over the cold war. But like any other artificial social construction, markets must be artfully used and carefully controlled; decisions as to what may be considered a market commodity should be democratic. For example, it has become painfully apparent that the earth ought not be considered a "natural resource" for economic exploitation. Further, people are not "human resources" to be exploited by the market nor should their worth be measured in dollars, as "human capital," subject to the market. Global markets must be coupled with global democratic political organization.

The expression "power begets power" unquestionably applies to modern corporations. On October 5, 1999, the largest merger in history was announced with the marriage of Sprint and MCI-World Com, this only months before America Online (AOL) announced its betrothal to Time Warner, an even bigger union. The deals were facilitated by the Telecommunications Act of 1996. Coauthored by the telecommunications industry and thousands of pages in length, the proposal contains far more than the deregulation commonly understood to issue from the act. Thus the Telecommunications Act has led to ever more powerful telecommunications corporations. Meanwhile, corporations use sophisticated public-relations techniques to convince workers and others that the market is a natural phenomenon, not to be touched, even as they manipulate and abuse the market to their own advantage.

Of course, corporations cherish aspects of the market that are to their own benefit, including those aspects salient in global markets, such as affecting domestic bargains on wages and work by taking advantage of the current mobility of capital, dismantling welfare states, undercutting social policy, and shredding the safety net, all of which derive in part from our global economy. At such junctures, and one would hope even before, civic society, democracy, and decency must challenge the undesirable consequences of corpocracy, indeed, corpocracy itself.

What happens to democracy, equity, freedom, and the economy when things go wrong? Paul Krugman puts it succinctly, summarizing the view of most economists:

> There are three things that macroeconomic managers want for their economies. They want discretion in monetary policy, so that they can fight recessions and curb inflation. They want stable exchange rates, so that businesses are not faced with too much uncertainty. And they want to leave international business free — in particular, to allow people to exchange money however they like — in order to get out of the private sector's way.[18]

It is generally agreed that although any two of these aims is possible, achieving all three is often unlikely (which is why Thailand had such a profound effect on economies worldwide). Krugman's point is that the global economic system requires active management. However, the authority for such management need not be left to the IMF, the World Bank, the Federal Reserve Bank, the World Trade Organization, NAFTA, or other organizations of increasing importance in the modern world. A preferable alternative would be to have the global system overseen by other organizational means or by existing organizations that are made more democratic. For example, in 1999 a mass demonstration in Seattle made public the existence and scope of the World Trade Organization, hitherto unknown to most. In significant measure, this week-long demonstration highlighted democratic control versus corporate control of the WTO. Organizations concerned with international trade should be combined with those concerned with international governments. Such organizations may be found in the United Nations or they may have to be created or they may emerge out of more properly political organizations.

Of utmost importance is that active management of the global economy be authentically and seriously democratic. Otherwise, to be blunt, democracy faces extinction worldwide. Controls must be expanded in order to protect the earth and its inhabitants, to compensate for the characteristics of a global economy that obstruct social policy, and to provide for democratic global organizations, democracy, freedom, equality, and social policy. Without such controls, the forms of social policy discussed in the following pages are impossible.

The practical consequence of this is that the adjustment of local systems is often an ineffective response to local injustices. Rather, such adjustment frequently must be coupled with a struggle for justice around the world. The time when political change within one country can be counted on to have a meaningful effect is past. It is time to think globally and to view possible and necessary acts of local progress, even resistance, from an international perspective.

# 3   Poverty

In the United States, a country with unequaled income and wealth, poverty is shameful. Such poverty constitutes an ethical demand for democratic change (the subject of chapter 10). Poverty is more intelligible when viewed in terms of wealth and high income. Most discussions of poverty do not address these, but here I propose to do so, first by noting that poverty is significantly a lack of wealth and income.

Wealth is the value of assets accumulated at a particular time. The wealthy have many assets under that special control called ownership. Disparities in income pale compared with disparities in wealth. In our economy, monetary income may be obtained in four ways: it may be derived from capital assets and their control; one may sell one's labor; it can be the product of public or private largess, policy, transfer, and the like; or it can be the product of crime, breaking rules, rigging rules, and so on. The first two alternatives are considered honorable; the latter two, despite the ancient notion of the "worthy poor," are thought to be dishonorable.

In the literature, poverty is almost always construed as poverty in income. Because income is measurable and quantifiable, it is understandable that it would dominate most of the social science of poverty. Although wealth may seem at least an equal or better index of poverty, it is usually more difficult to measure and sometimes it is even hidden. Have-nots lack not only income and wealth but also health, education, longevity, food, safety, housing, clothing, opportunity, freedom, and power.

The tenth "Human Development Report," issued by the United Nations, speaks not only of poverty in the United States but worldwide, where it is a

condition just this side of death, which is also true in certain areas of the
United States. The report states that development must include not only
rescuing people from financial poverty but also attending to violations of
human rights, lessening the disparity between the rich and poor, increasing
social stability, making people less vulnerable, and preventing environmental degradation. The report goes on to specify that such measures include
ensuring job security, housing security, and cultural security, as well as lessening crime, increasing educational opportunities, and exhibiting more respect for diverse conditions and needs.[1] Although all these measures are
indicators of what have-nots lack and what haves enjoy, most are difficult to
quantify. If this chapter dwells on income rather than wealth, it is because,
as mentioned earlier, most of the literature on poverty focuses on income.
Further, this chapter, as well as the rest of the book, largely concerns the
United States. Although poverty in the United States is less profound than
that in the Third World, its existence in this country is perhaps more shock-
ing and disgraceful.

Although poverty in income has long been with us, not until the 1960s
did Mollie Orshansky give our poverty line its official meaning,[2] in large
measure to fulfill the bureaucratic requirements of government programs.
Roughly, Orshansky defined the poverty line as a multiple of the money
required for the purchase of food. Thus larger families might earn more
money and still be poor, and the poverty line for farm families would be
lower because food is at hand.[3] Other reasonable variables may be added.
Heating costs are higher in the North than in the South; the cost of living
in New York or San Francisco exceeds that in Plains, Georgia, or Hope,
Arkansas, and so on. Orshansky had compelling reasons for not incorporating
such variables into the definition of poverty, as that would have made it
more ambiguous and increased errors in measurement. Although artificial,
Orshansky's definition is valuable in that it can be used to compare poverty
geographically and historically.

However, most people think that the poverty line is roughly half the
median income,[4] a higher figure than the official poverty line. Thus the
majority would claim that a family of four earning less than $17,500 in 1998
was poor. However, since median income, by definition, means that half the
people earn less and half earn more, the number of people in poverty will
always be a fairly stable part of the population, which is not helpful for
bureaucratic purposes that find it useful to talk about changes in the number
of people above or below the poverty line.

The concept of class adds another element to the definition of poverty:

power. Everyday language often includes references to three classes based
on income: the lower, the middle, and the upper. Because it is insulting
to be considered of the lower class, many in the bottom third of incomes
identify themselves as middle class. Because considering oneself in the upper class is perhaps pretentious, many in that category also call themselves
middle class. Thus most Americans refer to themselves as middle class, and
class delineations lose their significance. This very notion of class turns
from being a meaningful antimony between haves and have-nots into fuzzy
newspeak.

Much social policy is ostensibly directed toward the middle class. Because
Americans overwhelmingly claim to be middle class, a comfortable identity,
we may even be considered a classless society. In much American social
science, the number of classes ranges from three to five[5] and is formally
expressed as one's socioeconomic status (SES), a combination of one's education and income, which is somewhat redundant since each is measurably
related to the other.

A more historical concept of class is that of haves and have-nots. In a
capitalist economy, haves control capital and, through it, others who exchange their labor for income. This notion of class is directly related to
power, an entity that enters into any reasonable consideration of poverty.[6]
Extreme have-nots are those who obtain income through the largess of the
welfare state, charity, begging, or theft. Have-nots must settle for fewer important resources such as health care and food and must withstand igno-
minies like vermin and early death. Increasingly, extreme have-nots are geographically isolated. Physically separating off the poor makes it more difficult
for haves to understand what it means to be poor.[7]

In 1990 Kevin Phillips, a former official in the Nixon administration,
wrote a best-seller, *The Politics of Rich and Poor*,[8] that warned about the
growing gap between haves and have-nots. The warning was ignored, however, and today the income difference between the two has increased dramatically. (To a large extent, this is to be expected in a free global market
in which the winners do not compensate people who do not win.) Adjusted
for inflation, all but the income of the wealthy has either remained constant
or changed little. Record employment levels are coupled with a record number of poorly paid jobs, often without employee benefits. Many work two
jobs. The average American works sixty hours a week, a far cry from the
former forty-hour work week and the number of hours Europeans work.
Private debt is at an all-time high while private savings are at their lowest,

reflecting the vastly greater number of poor people as compared with the rich and powerful, whose incomes have rocketed, whose benefit packages are gift-wrapped, and whose personal savings (i.e., wealth) remain extensive even after the stock market decline.

The media's description of poverty is risky because the words used to represent the poor are often projections of class fears,[9] such as "lazy," "promiscuous," "dirty," "ugly," and "stupid." Among the middle class, such depictions confirm their difference from the poor and, to the rich, their wisdom and generosity. A seemingly alternative description includes such terms as "depressed," "insane," "dysfunctional," "unsanitary," "unsuited for marriage," "poorly educated," and "having a low IQ." This second list merely parrots the first but with fancier language that presumes to express open-mindedness, understanding, even compassion. Both are misleading and deceptive.

Perhaps understanding the reasons for poverty would help eliminate or at least reduce it—or so many texts on social policy seem to claim: identify the problem; uncover its causes; solve the problem. Policy rarely works this way in the real world. Indeed, the causes advanced for poverty are many and often contradictory. Poverty is overdetermined, and theorizing its causes is inherently political. To take an extreme example: poverty is said to issue from a lack of motivation. This bootstrap notion of poverty may coincide with the experience of our ancestors who, although poor, probably were able, by sheer will and effort, to change their own lives and the lives of their children. We are also told that poverty issues from a low IQ, an oversimplification of the argument expressed in *The Bell Curve*, which is an admittedly extreme view.[10] Or, as corporate-supported think tanks, pundits, or some academics would have us believe, poverty results from public policy like the New Deal and the Great Society, programs that made poverty more endurable and thus removed incentives for the poor to better themselves, caricaturing Washington as a center of evil ignorant of people's needs. According to this view, public social policies can only make things worse. Poverty is a private (even individual) problem that is best settled in the private sector (the market), which will solve it as it has solved the problems of the rich. These new myths have replaced the old ones, which claimed that poverty issued from sin, depravity, and promiscuity, and today are accepted by a significant number of Americans as the causes of poverty.

The secular causes of poverty are fraudulent. For example, although poor people are more likely to be malnourished and disabled, have poor prenatal care, eat lead paint, be exposed to toxic wastes—in short, run higher risks to their central nervous systems which can result in lower IQs—such poorer showings on intelligence tests are not causes but rather the results of destructive environments that many poor people endure. Thus rather than calibrating social policy to IQ, surely it would make more sense to change such environments into decent places to live. Further, the intelligence quotient is a measure of nothing so much as one's potential for success in school. Poor people are apt to attend poor schools or to participate in the poorer tracks of better schools; in short, poor people are less likely to receive the education that leads to better incomes. One's IQ is simply a number (unifactorial), and that one's intelligence can be measured by a single number (like an IQ) is suspect.[11] Also, the methodology of *The Bell Curve* is questionable.

Poverty and race are often intertwined, one often a code for the other. African-Americans are more or less of African ancestry. A serious argument about race and IQ would have to find that people who are more African in ancestry had lower IQs then those more European in ancestry. Otherwise, the argument is blatantly bizarre. (Indeed, modern physical anthropology has dispensed with any meaningful conception of race, regarding it perhaps as a concept emblematic of popular and media foolishness.) We must question the motivation behind any such study of race, as well as the motivation behind *The Bell Curve*. As Jean-Paul Sartre once noted, one would not make similar arguments (or conduct such studies) on the nature of tomatoes.[12] Nevertheless, all the arguments cited earlier have indeed been examined, a seemingly perplexing sacrifice of time and talent.

More respectable causes for poverty have been suggested, such as deficient schooling, race and gender discrimination, single-parent families, disability, poor health, violence, and drugs. Most likely poverty is caused by a combination of such problems, a combination that differs among people.[13] Were these explanations accurate, one might expect that poverty would have improved substantially even in the United States. Yet this is not the case. Indeed, poverty lingers despite these proposed explanations. Moreover, these causes are usually open to solution by public policy. Many emerge from studies funded by the public sector.[14]

Recall that although free-market globalization optimizes a narrow definition of economic efficiency wherein all nations are better off, in the sense that those made better off can compensate those not made better off, compensation is not guaranteed. Such economic redistribution is unlikely without guidance from civic society. Those who benefit most from trade are often and increasingly large transnational corporations. The powerful (frequently transnational corporations) rarely find meaningful distributions in their interests. Further, externalities and public goods (or "bads" like pollution) are often by-products of production. In a decent civic society, externalities could be internalized, public goods could be provided, and winners could compensate those who did not win.

Rarely do winners compensate losers, and often externalities and public goods are not taken into account. Indeed, typically they are not reflected in the prices that convey information necessary for economic optimization. For example, seldom do Third World firms include the costs of treating pollution, disease, and architectural degradation in prices. All this may vitiate even the economic benefits of free trade. Sometimes the explanation is obvious: a country may be threatened by a firm's relocation to another country. Corporate power, particularly of transnational corporations, is fairly constant. The power of Third World governments may be unstable, so the channels for corporate manipulation such as loans, bribes, and threats are likely to be broad.

Not only in Third World countries are welfare measures severely tested. Even in the European countries, once models of the welfare state and of the economic redistribution it requires, the welfare state is shredded by public, public/private, and corporate power. To fund its policies and programs, the welfare state requires redistribution, which may be accomplished by taxation, regulation, charity, or luck. However, the days when corporations, almost invariably the winners in international and domestic trade, have had an "altruistic imagination"[15] have slid through memory into distant history. Few corporations today see themselves as being able to afford "confiscatory taxes" or abide "bureaucratic regulations." Indeed, large modern corporations are likely to be even leaner and meaner, larger and more powerful, than before. They are more apt to be transnational, not only formally by expansion and merger but in partnerships and strategic alliances. Their expertise regarding their own needs is likely to find its way into laws, regulations, and administration. Upper-level management and those who run outsourced services like consulting, accounting, and public relations are liable to be former or future government employees or to know people in government. Not only is personal loyalty in restructured corporations apt to be minimal or absent, but large corporations have become increasingly prone to regard even mid-level managers as expendable. Political donations have become scandalous, congressional and executive branches often talking about the problem but never doing much about it.

Among the countless examples of corporate power, consider the following: "Out of 90 specific industry groups, none spent more to influence Washington than the insurance industry, which coughed up nearly $87 million during the 18 months through June 1998. A study by the Center for Responsive Politics found that 11,500 lobbyists for all interest groups spent a total of $1.26 billion during the same period trying to influence Washington."[16]

Or consider this: "Why do corporations pay $500 an-hour-and-up fees to Beltway lobbyists? Because lobbyists know how to pen just the right phrase and insert it at the perfect spot in a piece of legislation."[17]

Or for those seeking a business reference: "The committee system in Congress not only helps lawmakers to build reputations that attract increasing contributions, but also enables rival groups to focus their contributions on legislators receptive to their respective interests."[18] Is this not harmful to the democratic process and to social welfare and social policy?

Or from Capital Hill: "High-technology companies such as Microsoft Corporation are increasing their political presence through lobbyists and campaign contributions. This has eased passage of such measures as a moratorium on Internet taxes and expanded copyright protection for software and compact discs. High-tech firms remain largely unsubsidized and unregulated, but have formed such groups as the technology network to build relationships with policymakers."[19]

Or: "When a reporter asked President Harry Truman in 1948 if he would oppose lobbyists who supported his administration, the president replied, 'We probably wouldn't call these people lobbyists. We would call them citizens appearing in the public interest.' "

And one last example: " 'With MFN [most-favored nation status—W.R.], you have the entire business community 100 percent behind improving the relations with China,' says Ken Silverstein. 'I'm sorry to say this, because it sounds so horribly critical, but there is no way the power of the people can defeat the power of the corporate lobby when the corporate lobby is united. It just can't be done; there's too much money at stake.' "[20]

Given these reports of corporate influence and power over government, is it any surprise that corporations are sufficiently powerful to resist taxes, regulations, or other measures to alleviate poverty? Is it remarkable that corporations are able to resist redistribution (although they may not choose to exercise this power over redistribution from have-nots to haves)? It would be inaccurate to suggest that public policy toward poverty has always been in-effective, much less that it created poverty. Still, poverty remains. It appears instead that public policy has not been directed to the problems of poverty largely because of corporate power.

Economists divide the economy into three sectors: the private, the public, and the not-for-profit. In large part, the private sector, composed of small to large firms, is overwhelmingly concerned with maximizing profit, an alto-gether open goal. The public sector, in part, is involved in setting rules for and refereeing the private sector. Further, it is interested in public goods like education, law enforcement, and defense, which do not fall under the profit maximization of any firm in the private sector. The public sector ostensibly makes good on so-called externalities, cleaning up pollution, building infrastructure, even taking care of have-nots. As such, the govern-ment makes up for market failures in the private sector. The government, of course, is funded by taxes, yet in the global economy it is becoming ever more difficult to levy taxes against large corporations. Thus public policy in general, and social policy in particular, are increasingly funded by taxes levied on individuals, small businesses, workers in large corporations, and working have-nots. The smallest sector is the not-for-profit sector. Since con-tributions to the not-for-profit sector are generally tax-deductible (i.e., par-tially paid for by the government in forgone taxes called tax expenditures), the not-for-profit sector is significantly funded by the government.[21]

The three sectors often work together, but this occurs largely in the ab-stract, avoiding the reality of the role played by power. Traditionally, the public sector had the most power. The Declaration of Independence sought to establish "just power derived from the consent of the governed." As Lincoln put it, "[a] government of the people, by the people, for the people." Things changed, however. The term "private" came to apply not only to citizens but to businesses. With economic industrialization, power shifted from those who held land and property to businesses and corpora-tions.

Today the power of large corporations is unique and compelling[22] and is wielded over seemingly public policy matters. For example, a significant cause of urban poverty is a dearth of jobs in the city. Corporations have largely abandoned the urban areas where so many poor people live. Further, they lower wages by threatening to relocate. Even in those few cities with adequate public transportation, the working poor must pay for it in either money or time. The number of poor people exceeds the number of jobs located nearby, and paying enough to make up for job-related expenses is

difficult—this even at a time when the average rate of unemployment has
been so low. Some jobs are not mobile like those at corner grocery stores,
fast-food franchises, or check-cashing services. Such jobs do not pay well
and usually offer scant benefits. In short, the policy of the private sector was
largely responsible for the exodus of jobs.

Many inner cities have become poverty zones. Not only have suburban
shopping malls replaced downtowns, but many decent-paying jobs have
moved to the suburbs. A culmination of sorts is the "ring city," where services, shopping, and corporations have relocated to suburban rings around
the husks of once proud cities. The more progressive of such rings (like
suburban Atlanta) are establishing systems of public transportation so that
bargain-priced city labor has a chance to work in the suburbs. (This traditional role of public policy replicates the private van services Latinos use to
get from northern Manhattan and the South Bronx to jobs in New Jersey.)

How did this come about? During World War II, General Dwight Eisenhower was impressed with the German autobahn's ability to move troops
and supplies. As president, he undertook the interstate highway network, a
mammoth public program, the expenditures on which could be altered in
Keynesian fashion; it was a pet project of the automobile industry, big oil,
construction, and the many other interests that today form the core of the
highway lobby. The housing industry and developers profited. Today vast
developments spring up in a countryside once reserved for the rich, for
wildlife, and for farms. Years earlier, the rich had moved to the suburbs to
escape the infectious diseases rampant among their workers and the environmental pollution issuing from their factories. Then, as now, cities were
considered evil. The publicly supported interstate highway network transformed the country, enabling cars and trucks to drive reasonably priced mass
transit into bankruptcy.

To all but the many have-nots, the interstate highway network made possible what became packaged as the American Dream, a privately developed
home with a lawn and backyard where Mom and the kids could play, as
once romped the deer and the antelope. Such homes required furnishings,
appliances, and gardening tools, and were connected to the city by television
and telephone. The kids went to new schools, and, after school, patriarchy's
women drove them to Little League, Girl Scouts, and the homes of friends.
Women had to have a car, not only to drive the kids around but to shop.
Increased aggregate demand stimulated the economy in ways well understood. According to the Dream, two-car garages were desirable, since Dad

needed his own car to get to work. More Americans are injured and die from automobiles than from guns. Commuting is dangerous.

Not only was television part of the American Dream, but the American Dream was part of television. The air waves were given to private corporations that broadcast the American Dream. As televisions became cheaper (a fact not unrelated to their construction by inexpensive foreign labor), they were bought by have-nots to whom they offered expensive entertainment (and even more expensive commercials) for free. Have-nots saw the same programs as haves. They were sold the same products, although they often did not have the money to buy them. Easy credit made some available, adding to their poverty a shackling consumer debt. Thus have-nots were sold the same Dream, and not sharing in it could be a nightmare.

Suburban children ventured into the city when they became sixteen and got their own cars. Cars and kids, with or without booze, were recipes for automobile accidents, unwanted pregnancies, and a new dream outside the suburbs and in the minds of the Beats and blacks in various mutations, including the alarming rock and roll.[23] Eventually jobs moved to the suburban ring cities surrounding our grandparents' former factories, which led to a new form of urban poverty, one with spatial dimensions, a poverty unseen, invisible, onto which we could project our worst nightmares.

When President Eisenhower left office, he warned Americans of the dangers of a military–industrial complex. His warning has been ignored. It is part of what is more broadly a government corporate complex that led, inter alia, to the interstate highway network. Today, even beyond the lower costs of suburban housing, living in the suburbs often seems a rational decision for those wishing to protect their families from the dangerous terrain of poverty.

A sketchy account, but nonetheless, here was a new poverty resulting in part from public policy, in part from private policy, and partially from a mixture of the two. Poor schools poorly funded are another piece of the story. Policing by suburbanites is yet another. Add to this profiteering by slum lords, violence, and drugs. If there is a culture of poverty, it is because cultural adaptation to even the most horrible circumstances is a reminder of the human spirit. (None of this accounts for other forms of poverty, such as rural poverty, the poverty of those with disabilities, the disproportionate number of women and children who are poor, and the association of poverty with race.)

This brief tale is an example of the public sector and private sector working together. Such cooperation is an altogether accepted and open part of our economy. Far from being secret, here, as elsewhere, business and government proclaim their cooperation. Both the complexity and the frequency of such interactions have greatly increased. Further, as corporations became more powerful, business has become overwhelmingly influential in such governance appropriately called "corpocratic."

Not only is the private sector influential in conjunction with the public sector, but private policy is important in its own right. For example, corporate decisions to move operations, merge, downsize, outsource, restructure benefit packages, and establish work rules are all examples of private policy arguably more important to more people than public policy. For instance, General Electric's business decision to relocate operations have transformed Schenectady, New York, from a boomtown into a wasteland. A similar pattern characterized much of the Northeast. The mere threat of relocation is sufficient to hold down unions and augment corporate influence.

The not-for-profit sector is funded by endowments, tax expenditures, corporate donations, and personal donations, the source of funding perhaps an index to its allegiances. Overwhelmingly, not-for-profits are supported by haves, corporations, and tax expenditures. A typical not-for-profit has a board made up largely of haves and corporate representatives, imperiling charities not favored by such entities. For example, most chapters of the United Way have boards of haves who decide which not-for-profits are to be eligible for United Way support. Rarely are supported charities controversial. As corporate social policy replaces public social policy in the form of managed care, employee assistance programs, company picnics, and the like, social programs develop allegiances to the private sector. Changes in allegiance mean changes in values.

Although well recognized in the literature of public finance, tax expenditures are often ignored elsewhere. But not-for-profits can receive tax-deductible contributions that, by reducing the taxes a donor pays, in effect commands public-sector contributions. Thus public-sector support helps fund charities whose interest is only coincidentally on the public agenda and may even undermine it. Taxation is public policy, the Earned Income Tax Credit of 1993 having been the most important single measure against poverty of the Clinton administration. But the significance of taxes is well recognized by corporations that may have millions, even billions, of dollars at stake, that spend on tax lawyers, that may even have a hand in writing tax legislation. Of course, poor people cannot afford expensive tax lawyers (or often lawyers at all).

During the New Deal, the interests of poor people were powerfully expressed and heeded. Many New Deal programs were directed at poverty—indeed, had an effect in ameliorating it. During World War II, attention turned toward winning the war, an effort that created the military–industrial complex of which Eisenhower spoke in his farewell address. The increased production of military goods created a public demand in an economy where private demand had been lacking. According to principles established by John Maynard Keynes, increased demand led to increased production and the end of the Depression. As one by-product, the world war alleviated poverty, a significant Keynesian effect that also characterized much spending in the cold war. However, cold war prosperity left out certain categories of the poor, such as those who are poor because of discrimination, because of deficient education, the urban poor, and so on.

Today the war on poverty is history, having been replaced by wars on drugs, welfare, public schooling, Social Security, increased tax benefits for the wealthy, privileges for corporations, privatizing segments of the welfare state, and the like. The economy is becoming more of a private-sector economy, a fact indeed trumpeted. In such a private-sector-dominated economy, have-nots fare worse (including the working poor). The increasing power of large corporations over these years is hardly coincidental.

To a nontrivial extent, privatization, economic restructuring, the reconfiguring of large corporations, attacks on Social Security, the marginalization of the poor, the increasing gap between haves and have-nots, ecocide, although not inevitable consequences of globalization, are partially outcomes of globalization as it has historically occurred. The downsizings, abridgements of entitlements, privatization, reassertions of corporate power, and increasing gap between haves and have-nots are commonly attributed to the persons of Ronald Reagan and Margaret Thatcher. This personalizes history to an extreme. Although Reagan and Thatcher happened to be on watch, and although both look kindly on such developments, even had the personalities been different, the history would have been similar. Further, this peculiar version of globalization took place in other countries as well as the United States. Although globalization took a particular neoliberal form in the recent past, there is no logical reason why it had to adopt that mold. In human terms, there are many reasons why it should not do so in the future, a topic I address further in chapter 10.

In our country, neoliberalism was under way with Jimmy Carter, whose predecessor, Richard Nixon, had authorized the engineering of a coup against the democratically elected President Salvador Allende in Chile, now held up as a shining jewel of Third World progress, democracy, and social policy. (The role of U.S. experts in the reconstruction of Chile is typical. Although it is an exaggeration to claim modern Chile as the handiwork of University of Chicago economists, their contribution was substantial.) Transnational corporations exerted influence and power in all countries.

Conservatives, neo- and otherwise, often argue that public policy has only made poverty worse and will continue to do so in the future. Policy is to be left to what are held to be the invisible and impartial hands of the market, which overtake public policy, democratic politics, and civil society. It is important to distinguish such claims from our analysis. Roughly the conservative argument is that public policy is distant and bureaucratized, appropriating to its expertise decisions that ought to be left to individuals, localities, the private sector, and the market. The argument may be straightforward and simple, but it is wrong, even disingenuous. Many conservatives would forsake public policy for private policy, often a code word for corporate policy. The devolution of federal policy to the states makes federal policy inequitable (dependent on the state), giving corporations yet more decisive power over state government than they have over federal government. Programs that devolve to the state may further devolve to the county and private contractor. (The subject of devolution is explored in more detail in chapter 4.)

Historically the conservative approach to poverty was bravely attempted during the administration of Herbert Hoover. Enormous benefits were given to haves and corporations, and some of these benefits ended up paying the wages of have-nots. Anyway, have-nots who were truly motivated could work themselves into the openly government-supported ecology of haves. (In this, one may recognize certain striking similarities to the policies of today.) The New Deal was not only an attempt to cope with the Depression, but also an effort to cope with failed conservative policies. The New Deal recognized what had been acknowledged before and since: that strong government is the most readily available countervailing force to corporate power.

But what can be given can be taken away, which is now the case not only in the United States but in most of the industrialized world. A poignant example is the current dismantling of a once proud social policy in the nations of Europe. The mouths of gift horses bear critical examination to ensure that they are not Trojan horses: some gifts of public policy are welcome; others have welcome, if unintended, consequences; and still others, as in the Bill of Rights, shift power to the people. Below are only a few examples of beneficial public social policy, as well as beneficial private and not-for-profit policy.

Private policy's most important contribution was to create a level of prosperity that has turned poverty from a human condition into a soluble disgrace. Developments in Japan and the other Eastern miracles, whose recent economic troubles seemed to make some proud of our own particular path, are alternative ways to prosperity with different relations to markets. The road to prosperity has not been devoid of wars, domination over have-nots, and so on. Prosperity makes possible the amelioration, even elimination, of poverty, a far from trivial achievement.

Many sorts of public policy are more than partial successes of public social policy. These include Social Security; Social Security Disability Insurance (SSDI); Supplemental Security Income (SSI); Medicare; Medicaid; the Occupational Safety and Health Administration (OSHA); Worker's Compensation; the Earned Income Tax Credit; Women, Infants, and Children (WIC); the Wagner Act; Food Stamps; and Head Start. Such policies occur in the context of grander policies and often are not without corporate interest. Today such policies are frequently in political or budgetary jeopardy. But not to take such policies seriously is to put them into even greater jeopardy. For example, one of the most important antipoverty policies, Food Stamps, is administered by the Department of Agriculture. Food Stamps are different from cash, being vouchers for what the Department of Agriculture has determined qualifies as food. Food Stamps were initiated not as the result of the activity and pressure of potential recipients. Rather, agricultural interests—increasingly corporate agribusiness—pushed for Food Stamps as a sort of subsidy (as is much foreign aid connected to food). The eligible poor, however, take advantage of Food Stamps only half as often as is possible. This underuse is sometimes attributed to stigma, but an equally plausible explanation is the hassle of qualifying. Often, it is through the unintended consequences of public, private, and not-for-profit policy that the poor are affected, sometimes for the better, often for the worse.[24]

Those who grew up with the Warren Court may regard the Supreme Court—indeed, the whole federal judicial system—as a progressive force for democratic change in social policy. Yet historically, this has not been the case ever since Chief Justice Marshall usurped power by the Supreme Court to adjudicate the constitutionality of law in *Marbury v. Madison*. Later, the Supreme Court used the Fourteenth Amendment to justify the sovereignty of corporations. Currently it protects the influence of money under the First

Amendment. Further, it is ruling (legislative) law that protects people's civil rights as unconstitutional by a bizarre activist interpretation of an obscure Eleventh Amendment that views it as prohibiting citizens from suing their state. In many respects, we are returning from a brief sojourn in civil rights back into a customary world of states' rights, from congressional power to judicial power. A dramatic instance was the selection of a president by the Supreme Court in an unimaginable deployment of the power of the Supreme Court.

Policy is the precipitate of politics, and overwhelmingly politics issues from power. And, as we know, have-nots, despite their numbers, have the least power of all. It is not surprising, therefore, that public policy is rarely issued deliberately solely for their benefit. Instead, benefits for poor people are often unintended and accidental, serve the interests of the wealthy, or simply accommodate the haves' notion of the welfare of a society that includes have-nots.

Our society today is largely, unfortunately, and unjustly patriarchal. Most social policy, too, is overwhelmingly patriarchal and thus often easily and particularly directed toward women. The have-not status of so many women is an alarming index of patriarchy. Assaults on social policy as it exists in our patriarchal society often appear to be assaults on women. In fact, social policy is often paternal protection of women's space. However, such paternal protection is sometimes no better than no protection at all in a patriarchal society that is more protective of privileged men's interests than it is of women's. Further, paternal protections are particularly changeable by powerful patriarchal assaults. Thus the end of welfare was explicitly against women on welfare. The erosion of social security occurs when most elderly people are women and when women's care of children is complemented by their care of elderly parents. Assaults on much social policy for children are also assaults on the women who take care of children. Indeed, much social policy is portrayed as somehow feminine, often suspiciously so. Male public policy has more to do with macho deeds like war, commerce, and technology. Private policy, increasingly corporate policy, significantly replacing public policy, is self-evidently male, macho, and heroic (the hero being a male macho businessman, buccaneer, or entrepreneur). Or such is the common portrayal. Women are left with little support in a capitalism that impoverishes them, a bureaucracy that categorizes them, and a patriarchy that dominates them.

It is scarcely surprising that public policy complements private policy, that public social policy takes second place to other forms of public policy, and that often antipoverty policy is an afterthought. As is proudly proclaimed, our economy is a private free-enterprise economy, with other forms of even public-sector policies more important to it than social policy.

Haves are not inherently evil. Rarely is it their mission to make life as miserable as they can for have-nots. On the contrary, charity is found among the wealthy, although increasingly less by the corporations where they work. Yet times change:

> Former general Colin L. Powell is trying to influence corporations to engage in charitable works to solve society's social problems. These efforts may be ineffective considering that today's corporate leaders such as General Electric Company Chairman John F. Welch and Microsoft Corporation's Bill Gates treat charitable donations as non-essential costs to the corporations. Business and charity do not mix. Indeed, Gates has established a separate foundation to take care of philanthropy. The focus of most companies is to avoid takeovers and cope with increased competition due to globalization by cutting as much cost as possible, including donations. Charitable works are done only in a few places such as in Minneapolis–St. Paul.[25]

The modern capitalist system requires that corporations be as lean and mean as Scrooge. Further, charitable donations are apt to be deducted from workers' salaries in the form of United Way check-offs. Corporate-sponsored mentoring is generously donated by dispensable mid-level management under some corporate duress. The reduced amounts of corporate giving are hypercommercialized, the corporation often attached to the donation, and philanthropies funded by modern giants like Gates and Soros are kept apart from the corporate undertakings. Charity by the wealthy expresses their conception of what the less fortunate need. When too burdensome to haves, charitable gifts can be withdrawn. Further, haves may resent have-nots who show no gratitude for charity. Thus the benefits of charity to have-nots are not an unmixed blessing, as they are subject to the whims and power of haves. This partially accounts for why both public social policy and anti-poverty policy have decreased in this time of corporate power, where power is rationalized according to well-known principles articulated by sociologist Max Weber, including bureaucracy, efficiency, and interchangeability of labor.[26]

Overwhelmingly, modern social policy and antipoverty policy further the interests of powerful private corporations whose prosperity and economic rationality justify decreasing power for have-nots; locating have-nots in urban ghettos; privatizing welfare, Social Security, and health care; marginalizing have-nots; and helping corporate-influenced academies and think tanks.

For have-nots at least, entitlement has become an epithet. Volunteerism has replaced boosterism. Corporate power controls directly and through public policy. The United States has become a corpocracy, while the economic difference between haves and have-nots increases. A thousand points of light are insufficient to light up the skies, which, nonetheless, were illuminated around the globe by large corporately financed displays of fireworks, lasers, and flashes as we entered the new millennium.

# 4    Welfare

A remarkable change in discourse has occurred: the replacement of the word "poverty" by the word "welfare" to denote an American malady. Ironically welfare is not, or at least was not, the problem. Rather, it was an attempted solution to the problem of poverty. Of course, from time to time, solutions to problems become problems themselves. Indeed, a consistent conservative argument so finds an attempted solution to poverty: welfare. But something different is at stake here. In newspeak, welfare has displaced poverty in everyday rhetoric, the war on poverty has become a war against poor have-nots, and welfare reform means welfare repeal.[1]

As we have said, in a capitalist market economy, income derives from capital assets and their control, from the sale of one's labor, as a product of public or private largess, or as a product of crime, of breaking or rigging the rules. Income in exchange for labor is the most common of these: "As ye sow, so shall ye reap." Income by breaking the rules is more problematic, depending on what rules are broken and by whom. That will determine whether the problem is answered by the criminal justice system, institutionalization, or banishment—or sometimes it apparently needs no solution, being thought of as "just how things are." Income derived from the control of capital is different.

Certain categories of people are unable to work: in old English law, it was the lame, the halt, and the infirm (as distinguished from the vagabond, the beggar, and the criminal). In contemporary America, we do not expect children, the aged, and disabled people to work for their bread. All are considered worthy of our assistance. However, these categories are not firm. Whether one is considered a child is both a function of age and whether the individual is in school. For example, parents may claim children as dependents up to the age of twenty-five if they are full-time students; however, these children, at age eighteen, are legally permitted to vote and thus become civic adults. Eighteen is also the age at which they qualify as adults with respect to certain contractual obligations. Being old, of course, is a function of age. If one is of a sufficient age, one becomes eligible for Social Security. One may also choose to retire early, but with some financial penalty.

The category of disabled people is problematic. The state should provide income to people who are disabled, but the question arises as to who is disabled? Although an individual may seem disabled, that person is not deemed bureaucratically disabled if he or she works. The number of disabled people increases during hard times and decreases during good times, strange for a category that is often considered biologically immutable.

All these people, of course, are worthy of public support. All merit charity. Also among the worthy poor are widows, crime victims, war veterans, and those temporarily between jobs. All deserve pity . . . or so goes the myth. Apparently, says the patriarchal myth, a promiscuous girl who has allowed her hormones to rule her judgment, particularly if she is African-American, is worthy of help only if we choose to be generous. Thus she is not considered to be truly worthy. Her child, though, did not ask to be born. Hence former Speaker of the House Newt Gingrich advocated the beneficence of orphanages. Presumably, Gingrich reasoned, professional care givers know more about raising a child than underprivileged, promiscuous girls who think only about having more children. When many people hear the word "welfare," they immediately think it means giving federal assistance to these misfortunate girls; and thus, with these girls in mind, welfare was reformed. Some even think of these particular young girls whenever the welfare state is mentioned, although these girls are a minority of those receiving government support. More important, such support was a mere fragment of social expenditures, a grain of government spending, a trivial percentage of our gross domestic product (GDP).

Particularly directed at women, welfare is a product of a modern industrialized economy that requires that people be categorized, that the worthy poor be supported not only by family and charity, as tradition has it, but by the formal bureaucratic operations of the state. The level of support must be sufficiently low or punitively painful so as to make economically rational (female) people prefer work to state support. Further, the welfare state is supposed to provide, a social safety net to rescue worthy people in trouble through no fault of their own.[2]

Such people are often casualties of our economy. The solution adopted by the welfare state is to pay these people in such a way and such an amount that does not deter them from working. Particularly in Puritan moments, these payments are not above stigma and suspicion. The welfare state, in order to work, demands rigid categories that determine eligibility for benefits. Hence the importance of defining the term worthy," which, of course, is a subjective decision. Nonetheless, according to bureaucratic thinking, the term, however arbitrarily, must be defined.

Welfare, social programs, social policy in general, and our welfare state are understandable only in the context of globalization (as we know it). Social policy has been trimmed and cut not only in the United States but in Europe, Japan, and even in Third World countries and the former Soviet bloc. In certain measure, this is only a result of economic theory, as the mobility of capital makes it more difficult to tax corporations. In short, the Reagan tax and budget cuts were replicated in different ways around the globe. Cuts in pensions, health care, and disability support occurred in places other than the United States. David Stockman, President Reagan's budget director, reinvented a way to cut popularly supported programs by cutting taxes, thus forcing cuts in budgets, with propaganda spun accordingly, a mechanism favored by the younger Bush's tax cuts. In part, Stockman's reinvention was a necessity imposed by mobile capital, which could resist attempts at taxation by actually moving or only threatening to move to less punitive countries. This shifted taxes onto the middle class and poor, who often bore taxation with a resentment encouraged by the media. This much is traditional economics having to do with the mobility of capital as well as the effects of this mobility on the inclination of workers to seek more benefits and better pay.

However, the vastly increased power of transnational corporations affected not only the wages they paid but also government benefits and benevolence. The increased power of modern transnational corporations on governments around the globe assured corporate-friendly governments and, as a lemma, governments hostile to poor workers (routinely played off against middle-class workers and trade unions). In short, the influence of powerful corporations fixed the fate of social policy in the United States, including welfare policies and programs as we knew it.

The phrase "welfare as we knew it" is misleading, as most of us did not know it, being familiar only with media representation of it, maintaining a comfortable, though often distant, otherness. However, few familiar with welfare regarded it fondly. Experts devised schemes to modify or replace welfare. Many welfare bureaucrats did not like their jobs. The working poor often resented it. Few on welfare, contrary to the popular perception, liked it. Nor did most people like other means-tested programs such as Medicaid, Food Stamps, and SSI. Perhaps even less did they like the way these programs often worked together, sometimes at cross purposes.[3] Doubtless, conservatives are right that among the beneficiaries of welfare were intellectuals, bureaucrats, and case workers who made money through its management.[4] Add to this the unscrupulous medical professionals who overbill Medicaid, case workers who enjoy their power over welfare recipients too much, and corporations that count on a stable business environment undisturbed by starvation, infectious disease, and social unrest.

Surely it was time to end welfare as we know it. One way to decrease the number of those on welfare would have been to do something about the difference between rich and poor brought to popular attention by Kevin Phillips: that the distance between rich and poor was growing.[5] Although we have been in a period of slow economic growth since the 1970s, most benefits of growth have appeared in the pockets of haves (in part a consequence of the economics of international trade). The middle class often enjoyed this growth only if families could depend on two paychecks instead of what had been the customary one. Have-nots were more accustomed to working outside the home. Indeed, as middle-class women of domestic households entered the work force, female have-nots performed many jobs, heretofore without market value, such as working in fast-food restaurants (cooking), convenience stores (chores), day-care centers (parenting), and cleaning services (housework) and taking care of elderly or disabled family members. The differences between haves and have-nots increased, not inevitably as the result of some law of the natural world but by virtue of various decisions and policies, public and private, made or not made.

Similar changes occur in other developed countries. Particularly dramatic are the changes in the new European Union, where countries are scuttling welfare programs to reach economic consistency. Such consistency could be achieved at higher levels of welfare state benefits and protections, but they are not. The socialist regimes of Europe are hemorrhaging under an ostensible "Third Way" between free markets and centralized economies, this Third Way having received the sanction of European multinational corporations.

In general, Europe's welfare state looks ever more like the U.S. welfare state. The *New York Times* provides examples regularly: "Last month Chancellor Gerhard Schroeder of Germany laid out a radical agenda to slash state spending, freeze pensions, and cut the government's share of the national economy over the next several years, to about 40 percent from nearly half today."[6] That the European welfare state changes as does the U.S. welfare state is not a coincidence. Current global markets, as will those in the future, affect the hunger, lack of security, homelessness, health care, and stress endured by people both at home and abroad.

An example of a decision not made, a policy not undertaken, that would have affected income distribution and included those on welfare was a simple modification of the tax system. The government collects taxes and spends on a variety of programs, the budget being a more accurate indicator of national priorities than the State of the Union Address.[7] Some expenditures, like Social Security, Aid to Families with Dependent Children (AFDC), and SSI, are regarded by economists as transfer payments, essentially the government merely transferring money from one set of people to another. With some programs, such as Social Security, administrative expenses are almost zero. In a program with zero administrative expenses, the cost–benefit difference of a transfer program is zero. A deeper look at the cost–benefit difference takes into account the effects of the transfer program on paid work as was done with a negative income tax; numerous social experiments found people receiving monies from the tax system not typically discouraged from work.[8]

The effects of taxation on social policy rarely receive the attention merited. The tax code is unspeakably complicated so that only professionals, or those rich enough to pay professionals, are in a position to take advantage of it. Influential corporate sectors like tobacco, oil, and technology even influence the writing of the tax code. Indeed, individual corporations even have sufficient clout to insert favorable language into the tax code, sometimes of remarkable particularity, as well as to shape its overall structure. Although the government provides outright subsidies to corporations, often corporations prefer less visible subsidy by tax policy. During the Clinton administration, for example, taxes on long-term capital gains were reduced, numerous corporations were protected by import taxes or quotas, and the estate tax deduction was raised to $600,000 with yearly $25,000 increments. The Bush administration has eliminated the estate tax by 2010.

Proposals from the Right for a conversion of current federal income taxes into a federal flat tax, and other suggested "simplifications" to taxation, would further skew tax benefits to the wealthy and to corporations, as is openly discussed in the business press, although the schemes are likely to appear in the media as policies to alleviate the difficulties in tax preparation for all and even for the tax hit to the middle class, a term of useful ambiguity.

The Earned Income Tax Credit, signed into law by President Clinton during the early days of his administration, is a dramatic use of the tax system to benefit have-nots who work. Such use of the tax system to benefit have-nots was seriously proposed by economists as liberal as James Tobin and as conservative as Milton Friedman, both of whom received Nobel Prizes for other contributions to economics. Briefly, these proposals would have placed a positive income tax on wealthier Americans and a negative income tax on Americans who earned below a certain level.

A similar scheme was sent to Congress by the Nixon administration in a bill called the Family Assistance Plan (FAP).[9] Many who earned their living from the existing welfare system opposed it, as did other groups that found that the benefits offered to have-nots were too low. Others, on reasonable political grounds, thought that benefits to have-nots and children from an easily isolated negative income tax were more vulnerable to being decreased than benefits from a complex hodgepodge of programs. This political perception, however, became less relevant in a future where corporate influence increased dramatically and where few speak about poverty as a problem, preferring instead to speak about the problem of welfare.

Nixon's Family Assistance Plan went down to defeat by Congress. Many years later, H. R. Haldeman opined in his account of the period that the inner circle of the Nixon administration had counted on this being its fate, a fact withheld from Daniel Patrick Moynihan, Nixon's point man in the administration for FAP.[10] Only that segment of FAP applying to people with disabilities, Supplemental Security Income, passed into law. The eligibility requirements of SSI went beyond income to disability. If SSI had been part of FAP, SSI disability determination, as it is called in bureaucratic language, would have been a nonissue, FAP applying to have-nots, disabled and non-disabled alike. (Indeed, much welfare policy is disability policy.)[11]

If welfare as we knew it was repugnant to all, there had been many attempts to modify it. Medicare, Food Stamps, and SSI were three modifications. The negative income tax experiments were part of a new approach to public policy wherein social experiments were supported and evaluated in the field. The defeat of FAP was a setback to an idea that was proving itself in numerous real-world experiments.

At times, however, experiments were less concerned with rigorous measurement than in enhancing the life of local communities. The Corporation for Private and Public Ventures in Philadelphia, particularly when headed by the late Richard H. de Lone, was one particularly innovative endeavor. For example, in one of its projects, taking note of the resistance of building trade unions to nonunion entrants, de Lone matched a have-not to a master craftsman as apprentice. Such matching not only ensured that the apprentice learned a trade but also fostered a friendship between apprentice and master that helped the apprentice enter the trade union.[12]

Another experiment was the Manpower Development Research Corporation (MDRC). This project measured the success across many dimensions of various approaches to Workfare among several populations. Oversimplified, the results were that it could work for many people. MDRC, the Corporation for Public and Private Ventures, and other experimental programs involved money, of course, much of which came from a presumably ossified Washington.

By the time Bill Clinton was elected president in 1992, waivers from federal welfare mandates were easily obtainable by states and localities. Complaints about mandated central administration of welfare by Washington were misinformed, disingenuous, and partisan. In addition to various experiments by cities and states, federal programs were modified to include innovative programs such as JOBS. JOBS made use of federal waivers, and it subjected its programs to state-of-the-art social science analysis. One conceivable way of reforming welfare would have been to expand federal incentives for the use of alternatives to AFDC such as the negative income tax and Workfare, an incremental approach applying the piecemeal social engineering advocated decades earlier by Sir Karl Popper.[13] This was not about to happen.

During the campaign, Democrats and Republicans talked about ending welfare as we know it. Enough had been learned to make genuine welfare reform possible. After Clinton's victory, Mary Jo Bane and Peter Edelman were recruited to the administration. Bane had significant practical experience, having been in charge of New York State's Department of Social Services where Edelman had headed the Division for Youth a decade earlier.

President Clinton's administration started with a commitment to have-nots that spanned not only welfare but national health care and other less visible initiatives as well. The first tangible outcome was the Earned Income Tax Credit. However, the administration also took an aggressive stance in trade policy in accord with the protection of American corporations. The budget was altered to become more consistent with the demands of corporate power than with the needs of have-nots. By the time the national health care initiative was quashed, thanks in measure to the influence of insurance corporations, the two-faced nature of Clinton's economic policy gave way to a more consistently pro-business economic policy that continued throughout his administration. The power of transnational corporations increased, as did their protection and encouragement by a government increasingly under their influence. Indeed, we were not alone but were accompanied by the new Third Way in Europe, the new liberal "democracies" that we had encouraged or created around the globe, and increasingly large, powerful, bureaucratic transnational corporations.

Welfare held an interesting and rhetorically central position in the changes under way in the United States. All had come to a consensus, even before the election, about the importance of welfare reform. But welfare reform meant different things to different people. As a candidate, Clinton was too savvy a politician not to take advantage of the ambiguities and thus avoid pinning himself down to a conception of welfare reform consistent with that of the early days of his administration. Therefore, the Clinton administration was consistent in its advocacy of welfare reform, although changing what it meant by welfare reform. In its final version, welfare reform, as signed by the Clinton administration, was substantially the same version as that advocated by Republicans. Not surprisingly, welfare reform established a new bureaucracy of patriarchal incentives and disincentives, interfered in the relationship of have-not women and children, and further degraded impoverished women.

In a political coup that angered Republicans, President Clinton stole welfare reform from the Republicans. The administration delivered on its campaign promise of welfare reform. Unnoticed by many was that the version of welfare reform signed into law and the version the president had endorsed (tangibly in the appointments of Bane and Edelman to senior positions in his administration) was not the version of welfare reform he had campaigned on. Bane and Edelman resigned from the administration. Edelman did not publicly express his reasons until Clinton had won reelection, at which time Edelman wrote a scathing attack on the version of welfare reform that the president had signed into law.[14]

Welfare reform replaced AFDC by a variety of programs that highlighted a new program, Temporary Assistance to Needy Families (TANF). A not inconsequential aspect of TANF was that the mistake of putting three consonants next to one another, as had been the case with AFDC, was not repeated. Unlike AFDC, TANF was an acronym that could be pronounced as a word, "TANiF," putting it, along with many other acronyms, into the lexicon of newspeak.

The media image of welfare featured centralized big government that could hardly be expected to know nearly as much about local problems as state governments. Add to the already existing suspicions of big government the further mistrust that government was robbing the taxpayers through misguided social programs and the conviction that big government was cultivating a malignant subculture at taxpayers' expense into a cancer that would one day kill America. Finally, compound all this with the distrust that have-not women feel in a society dominated by powerful and wealthy men. To repeat, welfare, not poverty, was considered the problem. And like all problems, it must have a "fix" (a word added to newspeak by the Ross Perot campaign).

What was the fix? Set a limit on the number of years a person could receive welfare (like crime, welfare is not a worthy career); provide training for one of numerous, if low-paying, jobs; monitor programs more strictly, or, better yet, offer states incentives to monitor them so that only those truly worthy would receive assistance; provide day care for children too young to go to kindergarten, when the school system takes over the responsibility for babysitting and child rearing; encourage sexual abstinence; collect support from deadbeat dads; encourage state initiatives by the devolution of dictatorial federal mandates to provide democratic block grants to the states; and, finally, allow American business initiatives to fix the problem. Such tools were deployed in the replacement of AFDC, a revolution in social policy and a brave new experiment of dimensions not manifested since the New Deal and the Great Society. But questions remain: How long should the limit be? Should there be different limits for different people? Who should set the limit—Washington, state governments, communities, or programs? What about people still unemployed after the time limit expires? Should they starve, become criminals, or simply disappear? What about innocent children? What if there are no jobs or not enough jobs for everyone? What if jobs taken for those on welfare are snatched from people employed? What if the supply of cheap labor depresses the wages of the working poor? These are all significant questions.

And what about job training? Currently much training for low-paying jobs occurs in public high schools. President Eisenhower thought that Mary Switzer had gotten training right in her federal state rehabilitation program for people with disabilities. Yet how good a solution can this be if some 70 percent of disabled people are not employed, most against their wishes? Do we train for specific jobs or more broadly? Does being able to read help in getting a job? How valid are programs that largely teach how to look for a job? What about the costs of job training? If the economy provides many jobs, what happens when there is a recession? What is the place of public job creation? Should unions support programs that provide poorly paid replacement labor? Does getting a job mean forgoing Medicaid, Food Stamps, and the like? If so, can the prospective worker afford it? Can the worker also afford the time and travel involved in a job or in a job search? If not, who pays? What about unscrupulous certificate mills that undertrain, mistrain, or provide no training at all? Is a new apparatus of regulations required? Are we to expect that every woman should work? We have already reached a decision regarding children and the elderly. What about people with disabilities? And which disabilities are to be considered? How severe must they be? Who decides? And who decides who decides? Again, these are all important questions.

It may seem reasonable that states would know more about their own problems than the federal government would, but is this really the case? How does it mesh with economic globalization? Block grants to the states were consonant with devolution, states' rights, and the new federalism. Block grants allow TANF to fund programs at various levels and of varying sorts in different states. Whether these differences are warranted, indeed just, is questionable. Whether the "devolution revolution" eventuated in recipients receiving less is not so questionable. The argument is an old one that occurs frequently within a constitution that provides for the competing claims of state and federal governments.

The advantages of devolution of power to the states are at best ambiguous. The problem of welfare is less visible, perhaps eventually even disappearing into the niches of state government that also allows welfare reform to delegate many of its functions to counties, localities, and increasingly to the private sector. Traditionally, corporations have had more leverage on the states than on the federal government, although modern corporate power has been ever more successfully deployed at the federal and global levels.

Welfare reform was partially an effort to reduce the size of government. This aspect of welfare reform is embedded in a redistribution of power and resources. Although not part of political rhetoric, such alterations are consonant with the interests of corporations. Legislation concurrent with welfare reform had to do with taxation favorable to corporations and the wealthy, an activist Supreme Court, and trade policy that extended the power of corporations.

Should support come from church, state, or from private charity's thousand points of light? Who needs assistance and when? One hopes that people's intentions are good and that they are familiar with one another's needs and capacities so that the provision of support presents no problem. Unfortunately, the discussion of "Why welfare?" can rely on such a straightforward premise to only a certain extent. The truth is more complex, at times venal, and is usually consistent with self-interest—and rarely are self-interests unified in a society. When the state taxes some to benefit others, self-interests diverge; naturally some pay and some receive, one reason why those who pay tend to be critical of the welfare state.

For welfare to change in the future, for true welfare reform to occur, a renegotiation of power is required. Why is there welfare in the first place? Would that the answer to this question were straightforward, simple, principled, and predicated on that remarkably common code of ethics with which most people, barring untoward outside influence, seem to agree. Were this the case, the answer to this question might go as follows: life is sacred; society, recognizing this, and acknowledging that some people, for whatever reasons, are not able to survive decently, expresses its altruism by giving these people a helping hand, an ethical obligation in societies that have generated enough wealth to do so.

Having graduated from Dartmouth College, young Nelson Rockefeller went on a grand tour of his family's extensive South American holdings. Afterward, he summoned the leaders of the individual companies to what, were it a meeting of public leaders, might be called a summit meeting. He was troubled by the abysmal conditions under which so many employees worked. Crisply and authoritatively, he told the companies' leaders to improve working conditions. Were this not done, thought Rockefeller, workers might be likely to cause unnecessary trouble, trouble he would prefer buying off in the bud. Similarly, President Lyndon Johnson, when selling the Great Society to corporate leaders, noted that a wealthy country could afford the Great Society more readily than it could social unrest. Arguably, the vision of elites like Rockefeller and Johnson is what differentiates modern-day liberalism from conservatism. Liberals are more prone to pay for programs that prevent unrest, whereas conservatives are more likely to pay for social unrest after it happens—for example, by building more prisons or heightening policing. In other words, liberals prefer the carrot of incentive, whereas conservatives favor the stick of coercion. The last decades have seen the increased popularity of the stick, a significant part of welfare reform with the likes of time limits, enforced job training and job searches, and stringent record keeping.

Not that liberals are opposed to using a "stick" on principle. Nelson Rockefeller did so in his quelling of the prison revolt at Attica and in the Rockefeller drug laws. Lyndon Johnson used the biggest stick available to a president in his expansion of the Vietnam War. President Clinton used the stick during his campaign for the presidency when he returned to Arkansas to sign the execution order for a mentally retarded murderer. Sticks clearly are capable of inflicting genuine pain and frequently are replaced by carrots. However, all knew how to avoid the carrot for the stick when they reckoned it pragmatic.

Politicians want to get elected. Once elected, they want to be reelected. These two factors account for much of their behavior. By working for social programs, politicians earn the support of people who benefit from these programs, including those who work in them. They also earn the support of individuals who, despite their own financial interest, nonetheless favor some level of human decency. The modern conservative appeals to a constituency that is better educated, less marginal, male-dominated, corporate, more prone to use the stick in domestic matters, and wealthier. During elections, both liberals and conservatives move to the center, liberals confident of votes to the Left, conservatives sure of votes to the Right.[15] Some voters despair that there is not much difference between the two candidates, the accuracy of which depends on the meaning of the word "much."

With the expense of modern elections, which include television advertising, direct mailings, polling, and Internet maintenance, significant monies are required by all. Hence all appeal to corporations and the wealthy. At times, both find it in their self-interest to donate to liberals, but even more often to hedge their bets and donate to both liberals and conservatives. Gifts and influence go hand in hand. Thus, to the causes given for the end of welfare as we know it, we may add the corruption of the electoral process.

Understanding the distinction between the carrot and the stick is requisite in any society where there is radical disparity between the masses and the elite, between haves and have-nots. Indeed, one way to describe the welfare state is one in which using the carrot is the preferred approach. For example, in theory, substance abuse can be controlled by policing, heavy sentencing, even military intervention. Or it can be handled by prevention, education, following the lead of Nancy Reagan and Betty Ford, social programs, even taking serious actions against poverty. These more palatable approaches characterize the welfare state. In practice, carrots (positive reinforcement) and sticks (negative reinforcement) are usually used in combination.

The decades since the Carter administration have seen an increased use of sticks and a decreased use of carrots in social policy. We have spoken of a change toward the use of sticks in welfare reform. Compare this with Rockefeller's advocacy for South American workers and President Johnson's promotion of the Great Society. The Personal Responsibility and Work Reconciliation Act, of which TANF is a part, exemplifies a more sticklike approach to welfare policy. If one can ignore the ethics of sticks and carrots, as B. F. Skinner effectively did in his advocacy of positive reinforcement,[16] one response to a stick is not to move (the usual response to a carrot dangled suitably) but to cover one's buttocks or even to turn around and bite the hand holding the stick. In general, the stick is effective to the extent that one can control much of the environment. Thus it may work in disciplining children and wives with no place to go, on plantation slaves and prison inmates, but it is a more difficult tool to use in less controlled situations.

Carrots may be gold stars, high grades, bribes, benefits and privileges on the job, money, gifts, praise, public relations, or marketing. Indeed, such positive reinforcements can be more precisely controlling than sticks, disincentives, and negative reinforcements. But a problem with carrots is having enough of them and keeping them fresh. Sticks, on the contrary, are durable, reusable, and cheap—as is compatible with lean and mean corpocracy.

The sticks that pervade TANF include a time limit on benefits, new systems of record keeping and outcome evaluation, and the frequent conversion of jobs and work into punishment instead of opportunity. The invisible sticks designed to make one work in compliance with a particular program only ensure the *appearance* of compliant behavior by a client who can avoid sticks by acting compliant, perhaps under the eyes of an equally inventive supervisor who knows that the prime job expectation may be to ensure the appearance of compliance on the part of the client, the supervisor, the agency, or some combination of the three. Such acting may be viewed as good manners or fraud. Ironic, in the latter case, since ostensibly one of the purposes of welfare repeal was to ensure a decline in fraudulent behavior and an increase in personal responsibility.

Of course, sticks are cheaper than carrots, a simple truth recognized before Machiavelli and, in the Western tradition, demonstrated by the Pharaoh's enslavement of the Jews. For a while, as described by Michel Foucault,[17] the general use of sticks excited too many people to violence against their bearers, witness the beating of Rodney King that triggered a riot. Generally sticks are used in private, away from the scrutiny of others.

The modern criminal justice system is contemporary society's big stick. Whether prison helps deter criminal behavior is an open question. Yet, in principle, prisons could be replaced by preventative social policy. Indeed, the cost of such prevention may be less than the cost of imprisoning some 2 million people in what has emerged as a significant growth industry. To an alarming extent, social policy is being replaced by the criminal justice system (newspeak for police and prisons), as is further explored in chapter 9.

The evolution of the less obvious modern stick has accelerated since the Carter administration, with increasing poverty, decreasing access to health care by have-nots, replacement of slavery and Jim Crow by racism, diversion of resources from the ghetto to the corporation, and so on. An example is the improved technologies of policing, such as the development of nonlethal weapons like tear gas and rubber bullets, computerized technologies of identification, community policing (including increased vigilance against misdemeanors), geographic controls of violence, and the like. However, improved police technology, punitive welfare, prisons, the propaganda of old-fashioned family values (translation: patriarchal family discipline), the discipline of the market, and decreased public monies for prevention do not tell the whole story.

Today the middle class finds welfare threatening, but the burdens of welfare reform are likely to fall mainly on those have-nots who are the working poor. To the extent that welfare reform is successful in getting people off welfare into low-paying jobs, the current working poor compete for jobs with one-time welfare recipients. Such competition leads to not only a loss of jobs by the working poor, but often the withholding of benefits, wage increases, and improved working conditions. The use of public and private policy to set welfare recipients against the working poor may create resentment among the working poor toward those currently on welfare, kicking off possible new occasions for racism and ethnocentrism. At a time when our economy may be close to recession, such feelings may have ugly consequences. In short, the use of negative incentives in welfare reform threaten all have-nots.

Conceptions of unions must be rethought to include have-nots—that is, not only workers but entry-level workers, service workers, and people on welfare. Ethically a reevaluation is overdue; realistically the time has arrived; and politically it makes sense to include the working poor in unions.

There is scant evidence that most people on welfare find good or even decent jobs under the new economy, one that relies on negative incentives; rather, many end up on the streets, in the criminal justice system, dependent on their families, objects of private charity, or wards of counties with insufficient resources.[18] To grasp what has become of the welfare state, we must understand the greatly increased power of modern corporations and the massive deployment of ever more refined instruments, technologies, public relations, propaganda, media control, advertising, and the like. This increased power has been coupled not only with the impoverishment of many people but also with their disempowerment.

President Reagan's prompt, efficient, and ruthless firing of the striking air-traffic controllers was a public lesson to workers of what private corporations are increasingly able to do with judicial and legislative modifications of law. The displacement, or threat of displacement, of workers across increasingly meaningless national boundaries, corporate restructuring, downsizing, merging, the immense media profit tied to the Clinton scandals and other media events, the shift from the cold war into trade wars, globalization, and so on are all indications of the increased power of corporations and the downward spiral social policy has taken in our current corpocracy.

Although the business of running America has long been just that—a business—never before has the power of business been so great and so unabashedly proclaimed, nor have its connections with the public sector been so overt. The increased power of corporations and the enfeeblement of not only the poor but also middle-class people have created a new modern welfare state, one that is tough and carries a big stick. What once was benevolence from the government is now being reclaimed by an already corpocratic government that is increasingly under the control of corporations.

# 5   Disability

This chapter looks at disability policy in three ways: first, in its own right; second, for what it reveals about our welfare state; and, third, as an example of the many social movements that have advanced our country along the path from what *is* to what *ought to be*. We first sketch a bit of the history of disability policy.

Until recently, disability policy did not fulfill Lincoln's famous conditions for democracy: "government of the people, by the people, and for the people." Only recently did change in disability policy occur as a result of efforts of disabled people. Disability policy was fashioned by able-bodied people for disabled people. Even though such policy may be good, it is hardly democratic. Because this is true of most social policy that is fashioned by haves ostensibly for have-nots, disability policy epitomizes social policy.

Public U.S. disability policy was initiated after the Revolutionary War. A still unindustrialized United States seemed to take it for granted that veterans who were disabled while fighting for our country should receive some compensatory benefit. Indeed, additions and changes were made to public disability policy after most wars, even undeclared wars. Unfortunately, we have never done well by our veterans, disabled veterans included, particularly as the war in question faded into history. Meanwhile, battlefield medicine improved greatly with helicopter evacuation and, where needed, rapid transportation by ambulance-like jet aircraft to sophisticated hospitals.

Alcohol was no longer required as a crude battlefield anesthesia, at least for wounded soldiers undergoing surgery (although it is still sometimes useful, along with marijuana, heroin, and nicotine, to numb sensibilities in combat). Advances in medical, organizational, and other capabilities led to the proportionate return of more disabled veterans and fewer dead ones. As a result, the pressure for advances in policy for disabled veterans only increased. World War II and the police action in Korea led to the formation of rehabilitation medicine and a new profession called vocational rehabilitation. It would be cynical to view such progress as arising from the need to fight future wars; more likely, it arose from obligation and guilt. However, obligation and guilt are dangerous sentiments on which to rest social policy.

Other changes in disability policy occurred because disabled people are likely to be the children or siblings of able-bodied people who may have power. Further, although there is some substantial bias toward the poor, disability is not confined to have-nots, occurring as well among haves. In this, disabled people look more like oppressed groups such as women, gay people, children, and the elderly than they do African-Americans or Native Americans.

Special education was fostered by both the U.S. system of compulsory public education and parents of disabled children. Parents of children with mental disabilities were particularly active advocates, and some of these parents were rich and powerful. For example, celebrity Dale Evans, the on- and offscreen wife of Roy Rogers, was the mother of a developmentally disabled child; thus Evans's celebrity and money had much to do with the founding of the Association of Retarded Children (in our more enlightened age, the word "children" has been replaced by "citizens"). The federal Department of Developmental Disabilities was established by President Kennedy, whose sister was developmentally disabled. This department and state analogues continue, as do the Special Olympics under the support and supervision of the family of Eunice Shriver, a sister of President Kennedy. Other recent important disability policy was aided by Senators Lowell Weicker, Tom Harkin, and Edward Kennedy, all of whom had disabled family members. Such policy was fashioned for disabled people, often disabled children. Although such nondemocratic policy took on what political scientist Harlan Hahn identifies as "paternalism," it had the virtues of existing and being funded.

In the 1970s, Section 504 of the Rehabilitation Act and Public Law 94-142, the Education for All Handicapped Children Act, were passed into law. More recently, these have evolved into the Americans with Disabilities Act (ADA) and Individuals with Disabilities Education Act (IDEA). IDEA and 94-142 built on Supreme Court decisions that were to disabled people as the *Brown* decision was to African-Americans. Before 94-142, half the children not attending the Boston school system were disabled. If 94-142 and IDEA have not achieved the ends of equality of education and integration, they have improved public education for many disabled children. They were also significant in that they eventually generated a greater number of educated and informed students and citizens with disabilities, who increasingly seek participation in a society that still largely marginalizes them.

Section 504, known as the civil rights law for disabled people, incorporated wording from earlier legislation during the Johnson administration advancing the civil rights of African-Americans.[1] The ADA uses some of the same language as 504, as the latter has established some precedential legal record. Importantly, the regulations for 504 and the passage of the ADA were partially accomplished *by* people with disabilities, making this legislation the first major disability rights legislation with claims to being democratic.

Perhaps the most significant part of the ADA is that which prohibits discrimination in employment. The act prohibits discrimination against any "otherwise qualified" disabled individual. The wording is unfortunate because it has led to adverse court decisions and to a 1999 Supreme Court decision radically limiting the number of people considered disabled under the ADA. The ADA goes on to demand "reasonable accommodation" without "undue hardship" from employers. Not surprisingly, the courts have come to interpret these clauses in dollar terms. Further, the courts have had difficulty in recognizing the civil rights conception of disability that was part of the ADA's intent. In retrospect, the main function of the ADA may have been symbolic. It has established in the minds of many disabled employees and corporations some right to employment. Disability emerged from the church of charity into the arena of civil rights. If there is still a long way to go, at least some of that distance has been traversed.

Supplemental Security Income provides real, if meager, monies to people categorized as disabled. More money is available to people categorized as disabled under Social Security Disability Insurance. This provision of the Social Security Act passed during the New Deal provides money to workers who become categorized as disabled.

Worker's Compensation provides money to people disabled on the job. These programs are state programs brought into being by corporations to avoid the increasingly successful lawsuits brought against them by disabled workers. These programs were advanced on the state level in the old days, when corporations had overwhelming power only over state governments and were only just beginning to wield such power over the federal government.

We leave this sketchy history with a final note: that some disability policies make it advantageous to be categorized as disabled; for instance, discrimination on the job is actionable by a disabled person. (African-Americans and women have the same advantage, not so a white male.) Benefits from SSI and SSDI depend on one's disability status. Given the premise that people will not work without financial incentive, generally accepted in a society organized as ours is, and the existence of a bureaucratic welfare state that demands consistency of categorization, disability is valuable as a way to understand the structure of such a bureaucratic welfare state, a task Deborah Stone brilliantly accomplished in her book, *The Disabled State.*[2]

Indeed, it was as a consequence of three rules of social policy that the category of mild mental retardation blossomed into a seemingly scientific category. The first rule of social policy was the provision of free public education. The second mandated education for all. The third mandated that education proceed in grades. By itself, the second rule led to the category of truancy. The three rules, acting together, created a new category, retardation, which originally meant just what it said: being held back one or more years. Truancy, mild mental retardation, and IQ acquire their meanings by our system of free compulsory public education,[3] a system created by bureaucratic industrial society.

The disability category is derived from industrialized society by way of a bureaucratic welfare state. It is a premise often offered as fact: that people are lazy and will work only under the stick of coercion or the carrot of incentive, which today is money. Workers sells their labor to corporations, which have come to dominate our economy, in exchange for a salary. As Karl Polanyi notes, this reduces labor to a commodity.[4] Still, there are people who cannot work or whose work is not profitable to corporations. For example, being a child of school age is a socially acceptable and state-sanctioned condition to be unemployed. School age is increasing, in part the result of the global economy. To the extent that truancy leads to a life of crime, being in prison is another accepted reason for not being in the (ordinary) labor force. People over a certain age are also not expected to work, indeed sometimes not allowed to work. Pensions, Social Security, and Medicare are benefits bestowed on those over a certain age in an industrial, bureaucratic capitalist society. Land, home, and public ground are rendered into commodities, part of the more general artificial classification of "natural resources"; people, measured by their human capital and job fit, thus become "human resources."

The commodification and bureaucratic compartmentalization of existence is not without human pain. Disabled people, in particular, are often not easily transformed into the commodity of labor. Corporations have an interest in profit and labor, and hence marginalize, displace, or disregard disabled people or simply make them disappear. Thus disabled people, along with other "outsiders" (discussed in chapter 6), pose a threat to capitalism, to neo-liberalism, and to the large transnational corporations that benefit from them. As such, disabled people and other outsiders are existential proxies for human beings in general.

An important difference between the construction of disability by disability activists and the supplicant construction of disability by the bureaucratic welfare state is that the latter is a form of population control. Thus definitions created by the latter set a category of disabled people aside and categorically judge them incapable of economic contribution. As will become evident in chapter 6, varieties of the same construction are applied to whole categories of other people. Thus there is a purpose to capitalism's construction of outsiders in general, and disabled people in particular. Indeed, this purpose is so strong that it pervades much popular discourse about disabled people and other outsiders. Even when disability activists insist on their own definition, they confront the artificial realities of bureaucratic industrialism. Thus some 70 percent of disabled people are unemployed, and only 2 percent win lawsuits under the ADA, legislation presumably in their favor.

Other people fit into the category of the worthy poor, a category that evolved sooner than industrialism from a mercantile society. Today the worthy poor include the likes of orphans, students, old people, widows, and, of course, disabled people. Like the earlier categories, the decision of who is and who is not disabled, particularly by uniform bureaucratic categorization rather than individually, is made by the bureaucratic welfare state.[5]

Essential here is a definition of the term "disability," as well as an implementation mechanism connecting disability benefits, particularly SSI and SSDI, to this definition. Social Security Disability Insurance defines disability as the inability to work for physical or health reasons. This may seem straightforward and objective, but, according to this definition, the number of disabled people increases with bad economic times and decreases when the economy and the prospects for employment are good. Implementation is also difficult. Given the assumption that people are by nature lazy, the implementation puts the burden of proof on the disabled person (also true of many other supplicants of the welfare state). The determination of disability is made by a disinterested physician following standard guidelines. (Of course, physicians receive no particular training regarding disability determination, their training having more to do with treating diseases.)

Deciding what exactly constitutes a disability and whether an individual indeed has a disability is critical. Similar decisions, of course, hold in many other situations: who is guilty of a crime, who is recalcitrant, who is worthy of TANF, and, of historical interest, who was worthy of AFDC, as well as comparable decisions required of our bureaucratic welfare state. Such decisions require that the bureaucrat be suspicious of the supplicant, for there are incentives for the supplicant to act as if belonging to a particular category—as exemplified in the claiming of 4F status by prospective draftees. We are unaware of any acting students in one drama school who were drafted if they did not want to be. Of course, acting is not confined to professional actors. Thus officials must be wary of cheats, must even act in such a way as to anticipate acting on the part of a supplicant. In criminal law, this often reaches extremes, as in the cross examination, the third degree, and torture — presumably a thing of the past, at least openly. (Ostensibly criminals are presumed innocent unless proved guilty. Yet people with disabilities and other supplicants of the welfare state are presumed fraudulent in seeking benefits and must prove their veracity.)

In addition to policies assisting those who cannot work because of their disability, other policies help a person join the workforce. These are of two sorts: those governing the supply of disabled workers (who, upon working, become "cured" of their disabilities as far as SSI and SSDI are concerned), like special education and vocational rehabilitation, and those affecting the demand for people with disabilities, like the ADA. A definition of disability disqualifying one from work cannot be used to qualify a person for work. Still, there may be bureaucratic reasons to expand the number of disabled people. Thus states receive federal monies partially as a function of the number of disabled students, encouraging them to identify students as disabled. Further, special education has become a distinct industry, and its existence and growth depend on finding disabled students, discovering new categories of disability, establishing special university programs for special educators, funding federal grants for special education, and relying on the participation of special educators in awarding themselves these grants (a pattern familiar in other areas).

According to words of the ADA, "the term 'disability' means, with respect to an individual, (A) a physical or mental impairment that substantially limits one or more of the major life activities of such individual; (B) a record of such an impairment; or (C) being regarded as having such an impairment." Item C is an overwhelmingly important part of the definition, often overlooked by judges. Under the ADA, disability presumably approximates a financial benefit, as it requires some special attention from employers. And, winning a lawsuit, even those requiring that plaintiffs identify themselves as disabled, constitutes even more of a benefit. However, less than 10 percent of lawsuits are won, and 98 percent of cases under the ADA are never even brought to court; thus the rational disabled person, likely to be a have-not and otherwise vulnerable, is apt to think twice about suing and even whether to file an internal complaint.

To be disabled is to be stigmatized, marginalized, and often eliminated from the labor market. Moreover, the burden of complaints against employers, never mind bringing a case to a lawsuit, requires inordinate time and effort. Given these difficulties, a person would not likely have the incentive to be categorized as disabled. Yet, on June 26, 1999, the Supreme Court excluded from the ADA people whose disability could be compensated for. As expressed by the *Electric Edge*, the e-journal of the disability rights movement:

> The Supremes seem to have no clear understanding whatsoever that the ADA is about discrimination in employment on the basis of disability. Instead of recognizing that they're dealing with a civil rights law, not a benefits law, they fiddled around with ways to limit the number of people who could use the law, by trying to conjure up reasons to say they weren't "disabled enough" to "qualify" to even use the law.[6]

The plaintiffs in ADA actions consider themselves disabled and most likely are considered disabled by others (in accord with the often overlooked third ADA criterion of disability). These people claim a disability status of a different sort from those who would qualify for SSDI, Medicare, SSI, even special education. The ADA definition of disability is at odds with both the work definition and the school definition. This seems curious, since definitions are of consequence in a bureaucratized industrial welfare state; indeed, welfare states depend on uniform definitions. The curiosity vanishes, however, with the recognition that the assistance triggered and benefits offered according to each definition are altogether different. Our welfare state is really about two different definitions of disability.

Most public policy and private attitudes consider disability to be some sort of deficit or, according to the ADA definition, impairment for physical or health reasons. This is not the notion of disability held by disability activists, who define disability as a social and political construction.[7] The first generation of disability rights activists were participants in, or witnesses to, the civil rights movement. Most define people with disabilities as a minority, similar to African-Americans, Native Americans, gays and lesbians, and women.[8] Rooting disability in the tradition of minority groups and oppression was behind section 504 and the ADA. Further, regarding disability as an interaction with human and nonhuman environments was part of the ADA's intention, as item B and, particularly, item C of the definition make clear (and as the preamble to the act states). In addition, the ADA definition of disability emphasizes the person's interaction with society and with an ever more humanly constructed environment.[9] Thus disabled persons are not confined to wheelchairs; they use them for mobility. Disabled persons are confined by stairs (and stares), both socially constructed.

Many disabled people no longer attempt to disguise their physical difference. Accordingly, the disability category includes a host of different "lived" bodies that differ in different ways (the modifier "lived" being added to body, since difference often emerges only through the experience of living with a body). This manifests itself as a sort of disability pride (like black is beautiful) or as differences in the female lived body, not as characterized by men but as viewed by women themselves. Though this concept of disability as a different body is common in disability studies and is philosophically engaged by the branch of philosophy called phenomenology,[10] it has not yet, nor perhaps ever will, reach the status of law and social policy.[11]

The ADA and SSI work at cross purposes: the ADA enabling work, and SSI giving cash payments to those who cannot work. However, they are both constructed to demarcate a subset of people who may work only with some special accommodation. Characteristic of capitalism is that there is little such special accommodation.

From this discussion, one can well appreciate the importance of categorization and definition to disability and disability policy, to disability activism, and to the contemporary bureaucratic welfare state, which has analogous problems defining such other categories as the unemployed, suspect classes, felons, immigrants, the mentally ill, criminals, drug addicts, and other outsiders. Such problems are encountered in bureaucracies that demand equality of treatment, interchangeability of supplicants, and domination of supplicants. How the family of a disabled person considers disability, for example, may well differ from a bureaucracy's view; it may be more customized, more changeable, and more interactive (to the degree that the family is independent of public and private bureaucracy). Corporate capitalism does not and cannot as readily adapt to the needs and contributions of a person with a disability, one reason why corporations are often hostile to the ADA.[12]

The modern category of disability is constructed by bureaucratic capitalism, as, indeed, is our welfare state. In fact, the two competing definitions of disability, as a minority and as a supplicant category, are the same to bureaucratic capitalism. Capitalism's interest in people is overwhelmingly as consumers and workers. Although capitalism is starting to see disabled people as a niche market served by professionals and even by standard products involving some token effort to cultivate disabled people as consumers, capitalism's main interest in disabled people, as in other outsiders, is as problematic labor. It is not in the interest of bureaucratic capitalism to fit the job to the person, except in the token ways advanced by the ADA as "reasonable accommodation" without "undue hardship."

Although, in principle, a job can be broken down in many ways, as is recognized in modern business literature under the rubric "job analysis," it will hardly do for corporations to continually alter job analyses according to the different requirement of differently disabled people. In this, bureaucratic capitalism is exquisitely different from family, farm, and other nonbureaucratic, noncapitalist organization. Thus bureaucratic capitalism constructs its distinctions according to whether a person can work within already given job structures. Disabled people cannot, except for a minority lucky enough to find an accommodating job, willing to work that much harder, and open to taking a lower-paying job.

Ultimately, disability is constructed in such a way as not to cause bureaucratic capitalism "undue hardship." From the categories of capitalism come the realities of work and much of the rest of life. These are secondary to the interests of capitalism, not only for people with disabilities but for other outsiders such as criminals, institutionalized people, and even usual workers. In short, disability highlights a situation in which labor and human beings are viewed as human capital or as commodities.

That the categorizations of the modern bureaucratic welfare state, including disability, echo those of bureaucratic capitalism is no surprise, since our welfare state is an adjunct to capitalism. Furthermore, the categorizations of corporate America penetrate childhood and families (one of whose functions is to socialize the child to work), social banter ("What do you do for a living?"), and law. Indeed, work and categorization are central to our capitalist society, as is categorization according to actual or predicted ability to work; the extra bother attendant to not individualizing uniform bureaucratic rules and not regarding people as human beings in other fashions are only to be expected in our bureaucratic capitalist society. Those wishing further clarification, if with a different slant, are referred Deborah Stone's *The Disabled State*.[13]

What of charity (what Tennessee Williams called "the kindness of strangers"), caring, sympathy, noblesse oblige? Surely disabled people, among supplicants of the welfare state, have received such expressions of charity in exemplary amounts. Charity differs from rights. In discussing this difference, one is well advised to attend to depictions of people with disabilities in the (able-bodied) media.

In literature and drama, the lived human body is sometimes used to represent invisible spirit, personality, intent, and morality.[14] For English speakers, the most obvious example is Shakespeare's Richard III, whose hunchback makes visible the deformities of his soul. Shakespeare has Richard III speak to the putative connection between physical and moral deformity. What of Dickens's Tiny Tim? His disability makes him a perfect object of Christmas pity. Our hearts go out to him, as surely as do our donations to the equally unfortunate children Jerry Lewis sponsors. Captain Ahab's prosthesis embodies more than evil; it also symbolizes a defiant humanity against nature. Unlike Richard III and Tim, we know that Ahab and Captain Hook were once victims of nature, which perhaps is intended to justify their actions against others, even against children. Contemporary media, plays, and movies—for example, *Children of a Lesser God*, *Wait Until Dark*, and *The Miracle Worker*—portray the heroic ability of the human spirit to overcome a physical disability by undergoing an extreme form of rehabilitation. Yet, while admiring their actions, one cannot help but think: "There but for the grace of God go I."

The expression "There but for the grace of God go I" characterizes other supplicants of the contemporary welfare state, even those who are simply unemployed. Obviously, disability is undesirable and to be overcome, cured, or otherwise transcended. Those with disabilities need our sympathy, even our charity. Entertainment challenges us to help: the modern telethon by Jerry Lewis, solicitations at movie theaters for the Jimmy Fund, and many other charity appeals augment our actions of charity.[15] Similar appeals are made to the thousand points of light for other supplicants of the welfare state. A correlate to this must be that the welfare state is not doing its job and must be helped or replaced by private charity.

In a society dominated by haves, in which charity is an afterthought to remedy unfortunate disasters, in which charity is frequently linked to gratitude and obedience, we must look gift horses in the mouth. Our Declaration of Independence did not ask for the charity of the Crown but declared our independence and expressed our rights. Ever more responsive to its share holders and responsible to the bottom line, a modern corporation can less afford to be charitable than older counterparts, which could reckon charity as a benign inefficiency. The growing privatization of the welfare state makes of public rights private charity. The inefficiency of such a system is more than made up for by the reduction of resources for programs of the welfare state. Charity erodes rights, enhances the power of haves, and degrades have-nots. A society in which begging is required for survival is not a decent society.

Recently, we have witnessed a new American creation: the disabled celebrity. A deaf Miss America tells us that anything can be accomplished with God's help. Further, a first-rate actor, Christopher Reeves, synonymous to many as Superman, one of his major roles, falls from a horse and becomes a quadriplegic. This was a tragedy, of course, considered by many a fate worse than death, a view Reeves no doubt held, if only momentarily, in his rehabilitation, but with which he now disagrees. Despite his disability, he remains a celebrity, even breaking new ground. His message is of a future cure for those with spinal cord injuries. One may infer, of course, that this promise of cure holds for other disabled people as well.

For Reeves, disability is something to escape. He has been successful in drawing attention and dollars to that escape, which fits the disability myth. Unfortunately, he speaks little of his professional achievements, which continue; of his loving friends and admiring fans; of his access to the best. We are left with the standard disability myth and the standard myth of welfare state supplicants. Few disabled people are superstars.

Telethons are rituals in which participants feel good about themselves,[16] a have-nots' version of galas enjoyed by the wealthy, as, for example, when a rich person makes it into society by donating significant treasure to an art museum. Telethons and donations to art museums eventuate in private re-sources being transferred to places where they arguably will do good. Still, the donation to the museum involves a significant tax expenditure by the government to finance a new arrival, and if telethons may attract needed money not forthcoming from the welfare state, it arrives less efficiently and with debilitating corrosion of the worthiness of supplicants.

It is not that charity from President Bush the elder's thousand points of light may not help both the recipient and the donor. It is not that giving to charity is not worthy, although economist Milton Friedman holds that it is not a proper role for corporations. But even a thousand points of light are insufficient to illuminate the world of have-nots. Indeed, haves' actions in areas other than individual charities raise questions regarding the nature of their desire to help the less fortunate. Moreover, charity is not a right, and to the extent that charity replaces rights, it replaces citizens by supplicants.

The sociologist Erving Goffman suggests that the function of his version of the disability category—a version he calls "stigma," which also exists with some other supplicant groups—may be to distinguish people so categorized on the marriage market.[17] Modern studies show, however, that in our patri-archal society male power and wealth are more important than a man's physical attributes, whereas, for men, women's most valuable attributes are beauty, sexuality, and charm. This sexist division ought not distract us from the observation that power and wealth speak directly to the have/have-not categories. This leaves significant questions about disabled women, ques-tions whose answers remind us that sexism is alive and well. Although the gender category is much like the disability category and other supplicant categories, gender does not simply add to these categories, but complicates and augments these other supplicant categories. Male disability is a social category framed by work. An able-bodied person is expected to work during the working age; a disabled male is not. Bureaucratic capitalism finds such gross distinctions less problematic than personal distinctions for each "case."

Earlier in this book, the discussion of categories focused on the categories themselves rather than on their genesis, effect, and consequence. Categories of disability are immediately striking and expose the nature of social policy, the supplicant category, and the relation of both to the economy. Here, as elsewhere, public policy is less important than private corporate policy, which constructs many of the attitudes, categories, and actions of public social policy. Regarding not-for-profit policy for disabled people, as for other have-nots, although its motives may be good, it can be withdrawn, since charity is not a right. Further, not-for-profit policy here, as in many other areas for have-nots, reinforces the asymmetric power relationship between haves and have-nots. Finally, not-for-profit agencies compete with one another for fixed monies. This requires inordinate time and attention, and forces groups of have-nots to compete with one another as well. Not-for-profit policy for disabled people is similar to other not-for-profit policy for have-nots.

Private policy sets the categories for public social policy. Our discussion turns now directly to private policy, which has made of human labor a commodity and has created "human resources." Modern economics quantifies, measures, and otherwise uses this commodity, which it calls "human capital."[18] What may have seemed arch when President Calvin Coolidge divulged it—that "the business of America is business"—is now taken for granted, at least by the more extreme haves. As businesses have turned more into bureaucratic capitalist corporations, and as corporations have grown, flourished, and prospered, they have come to influence more of American policy, media, culture, education, and thought. The corpocracy has come of age.

Globalization has affected disability by reducing the monies distributed to people under social policies such as SSI, SSDI, special education, and vocational rehabilitation. Further, although we expected the opposite of our "information economy," it has reduced the number of decent jobs available to disabled people. A reactionary Supreme Court is putting the Americans with Disabilities Act through a judicial shredder. Even before decisions reinterpreting the Eleventh Amendment as being against individual rights and for states' rights, a view of disability that finds it incompatible with work (a view explicitly not intended by the drafters of the ADA) and other attacks on social policy that include people with disabilities, the modern Supreme Court, acting often in conformity with a corporate global economy, appropriate for a judicial branch that gave corporations the rights of people, usually enlarges the privileges of corporations and has indeed created the modern immortal sovereign American corporation.

The Supreme Court has been asserting its power before it went public in selecting the younger George Bush for president. It has denied Congress the authority to insist on civil rights over states' rights by using the Eleventh Amendment in a fashion that shows that inventing rather than interpreting the Constitution is not a prerogative of liberal courts. Before acting against the ADA in *Garrett v. University of Alabama*, it acted against labor in *Alden v. Maine* and against the elderly in *Kimmel v. Florida Board of Regents*. The future only promises a more active, reactionary, and powerful Court.

The interaction of corporations with disabled people is not traditionally spoken of as social policy. But disabled people are profoundly affected by corporations, which may design products for standardized able bodies and may discriminate against disabled people as workers because of bigotry, profitability, and expense or because the thought of hiring a disabled person as a worker has simply never occurred. Further, people with disabilities have a particular relationship to the modern corporation, which demands of people that they be as interchangeable as parts are for factories. The bureaucracies that are so much a part of modern corporations demand interchangeability of people not only on the assembly line but throughout the bureaucracy.

In large corporations, job analysis is outsourced or performed in-house by specialists whose job descriptions presumably include the ability to perform job analyses. In principle, there are many ways to organize the labor necessary for production. The way that is chosen is a function of technology, product, organizational environment, human capacity, efficiency, and control. Yet even human capacity is not related to existential human reality but to human beings as used by corporations, the commodity of labor. Indeed, large corporations have departments called Departments of Human Resources. As with natural resources and the earth, human resources presuppose labor to be a commodity.

Women are overrepresented in the upper positions of human resource departments, perhaps because of patriarchal conceptions of women as intuitive, nurturing, and caring. Human resource departments bend these sexist attributes to the needs of the patriarchal bureaucratic corporation. Further, these departments enjoy the lowest prestige of all corporate departments. What does this imply for people with disabilities? The pretense of reasonable accommodations, even including minor modifications to job descriptions, are in some way considered, if only to be rejected by the instrumental patriarchal bureaucracy of the corporation. More significant, job analyses are designed based on the capacities of able-bodied workers and constitute the first barrier to disabled workers (nonworkers?) in bureaucratic capitalist corporations, which today may have "flatter" bureaucracies and be more flexible but are bureaucracies nonetheless.

Bureaucratic capitalism does not hire people; it hires the commodity of labor, increasingly interchangeable labor. This is particularly difficult for many disabled people who, although, in principle, may be good workers at a company, in fact may not be considered so because the work they can do, while useful and necessary, does not fit bureaucratic job analyses. (The ADA tries to remedy this in its reasonable accommodations language.) Bureaucratic interchangeability is hard for nondisabled people as well. It wears them out, burns them out, and drives many to the health and mental health systems. Corporate bureaucracies recognize this and promote stress-reduction programs, company parties, banquets and picnics, employee-assistance programs, bonuses, and better food in the cafeteria. They also encourage employee "input," and thus recognition of a worker by management. Despite this, a recent study found 25 percent of people angry with their jobs, a situation to be remedied with greater recognition of workers by management.[19] The disabled persons' inherent resistance to bureaucratic interchangeability is thus only an extreme form of human resistance and alienation. However, since it has as a consequence that some 70 percent of disabled people are unemployed and even more are underemployed, the effects of such bureaucracy are clearly destructive.

The welfare state complements the private sector, now largely corporate. One "commodity" used in production is labor. Corporations have a direct interest in making the transition from one job to another bearable. This contribution to "labor flexibility" is facilitated by public policies like unemployment insurance. Many sorts of labor are simply too problematic, however. Corporations need not think about hiring the almost 2 million prospective employees who populate our prisons. Of course, this does not obviate the profitable outsourcing of some production to the prisons, increasingly private. Schools function to make students think corporate, obey rules, learn skills, and otherwise increase their value as human commodities. Few people want to work past retirement age, Social Security making for a less restive labor force. Since Social Security encourages a troublesome unity among generations of workers, corporations have an interest in both decreasing and privatizing it.

In general, the categories of the bureaucratic welfare state protect bureaucratic capitalist corporations; nonetheless, these corporations wish to narrow these categories and decrease the amount of public monies used under the guise of freedom of choice by reducing taxes to benefit corporations and the wealthy. This desire, discussed with regard to welfare, Social Security, and health care, holds for people with disabilities as well.

If the future echoes the present, privatization, lower funding levels, and more narrowly drawn categories of the worthy and nonworthy poor are to be expected. Aid to Families with Dependent Children, substantially a disability program, has been axed. The monies per capita for disabled people have decreased both in vocational rehabilitation and special education despite a growing class of professionals. One might expect that the not-for-profit sector in disability would blossom given increased corporate wealth and the growing wealth of haves. In fact it has, but not as much as might be expected. Fewer public funds are available today, and more not-for-profits compete vigorously for finite private personal donations and corporate underwriting. Indeed, the profession of begging has changed remarkably, and capable grant writers are much in demand.

It is significant that the more that democratic elements of public disability policy have progressed, the less common it is to dismiss disabled people as subhuman, as once was fashionable. Today disabled people are listened to, if not heard, by public policy makers. A new larger cohort of disabled citizens has emerged from the educational system. The ADA was a revolutionary, if overdue, law, which nonetheless is under full attack in the courts. The 70 percent unemployment rate is only one index of the continuing disgraceful status of people with disabilities.

Still, being disabled today is easier than it was yesterday. Disability activists were correct in finding disability a social and political construction. Democratic public policy fashioned not only for disabled people but by and of them is more difficult to reverse. Democracy is more reliable than charity.

# 6  Social Security

Social Security is the symbolic centerpiece of our welfare state. Occasionally we shall be critical of it and of the motivations that created and sustain it, but it is essentially a good program. Social Security not only is symbolically central, but is central to the domestic social policy budget. Some speak of social policy as constituting the largest chunk of public policy. This is true if, and only if, Social Security is included. Without it, public social policy becomes far more peripheral. Indeed, this budgetary importance contributes to Social Security's symbolic importance. Given this, it is astonishing that our welfare state's public policy of Social Security is as new as the New Deal. It is difficult to imagine this country without it. Stretching the imagination is always a valuable effort, indeed necessary for future social progress. Before Social Security, to become (sixty-five years) old, particularly for have-nots, was to lose one's income. Haves who lost work lived off their wealth, including pensions, that they had accrued during a life of high income, quite possibly with significant benefits. Not true of have-nots.

For have-nots, the loss of a job meant a loss in income that often meant destitution. The impoverished elderly are not particularly adept at street crime. Few will buy their labor, and they have few, if any, assets on which to live. Further, their health is likely to be worse than those who are younger. Indeed, the poverty of old age contributes to poor health in one of the many small vicious circles found in the arena of social policy. Some old people crumple up and die. Others survive with help from their children, their church, charity, or just plain luck.

Couples often decide to have many children not only to compensate for those possibly lost to the ravages of childhood infectious diseases but as an investment in their future. If enough children survive into their parents' old age, they will be around to take care of their parents. Birth rates have decreased in those Third World countries that have developed economically. Where once it was thought that poverty was the result of having too many children, the reality is more complex, higher standards of living and education leading to women having fewer children. (Indeed, in this country, having children is usually an economic loss, as discussed in chapter 8.)

Before Social Security, old people were often at the mercy of either their children's kindness or the kindness of strangers. The high probability that have-nots would work all their lives, contribute to the country's moral and financial wealth, and be paid back, at best, by dependents or charity and, if not, by poverty, homelessness, and premature death was blatantly repulsive. Before Social Security, the pauper's grave was a common destination.

From a cynical view, living to be old enough to collect Social Security was rare at the time of the New Deal, particularly among have-nots. Indeed, Social Security was not a policy targeted at have-nots. And the promise of even a meager pension at old age might have been recognized as contributing to spending, which would have helped stimulate the economy. This, however, would have been an accidental effect of Social Security, some unconscious Keynesian economics. Although true, these observations are as irrelevant to Social Security as they became to less recognized parts of Social Security, its insurance aspects. They included insurance against disability (Social Security Disability Insurance) and what was, in effect, a form of insurance against poverty (Aid to Dependent Children, later changed to Aid to Families with Dependent Children). Nor does such cynicism recognize that Social Security was also a tree on which ornaments such as Medicare, Medicaid, and Head Start could later be hung. Finally, cynicism does not deal with Social Security and its progeny being entitlements, many not even means-tested. Much later, Wilbur Cohen, ultimately to become head of the Social Security Administration, would observe that programs for poor people tend to be poor programs, generally a true observation in a welfare state created by haves.

Motives should not be mistaken for effects, and the consequences of Social Security were initially good and were to become better. Universally entitling people to social claims on resources was in itself a good thing, and added to this was an enormous consensus built up for Social Security that could not easily be taken away. This was true even of the means-tested parts such as AFDC, which was to become more controversial but was to remain in place until the repeal of welfare as we knew it during the Clinton administration (see chapter 4). This is remarkable since the first Social Security system was put in place in the nineteenth century by the conservative German Bismarck regime, not even reaching this country until the New Deal. Social Security promised all people, haves and have-nots, that they would not become paupers at old age from losing their income upon retirement. True, when the measure was passed, few people survived to collect Social Security, and even today the working poor pay proportionately more money into the system than they collect when they become eligible for Social Security benefits, partially because the Federal Insurance Contributions Act (FICA), the tax that funds Social Security, is not overly progressive, but also because the life expectancy of have-nots is lower than that of haves.

If Social Security does not make income equal among the elderly, it does make the elderly's income more nearly equal to those in the workforce. Significantly, it enables the elderly to share a similar political and economic interest, often translated into political power. Indexed to inflation, Social Security benefits have relieved many old people from the fear that they would be a financial burden on their children. Moreover, it has low administrative costs.

On a rainy night on the Lower East Side of New York, an old man emerged from a then cheap Odessa restaurant, literally singing in the rain, something more expected from young people in Hollywood movies. "Why are you singing?" a young man (the author) asked, perhaps in a moment of youthful grumpiness. "What's not to sing about? Today I got my Social Security check. I paid my rent. I bought food. My belly is full. I am a happy man. A happy man should sing." Of course he should, and a young man should not be grumpy just because it is raining. Perhaps the old man was happy by nature, but, even so, his song was also a hymn to Social Security. There was dignity to the old man, and partially it was the dignity of Social Security (Old Age Survivors and Disability Insurance [OASDI]), part of the social contract our country has with old people who have worked.

Families of workers who die early are also eligible for Social Security benefits, a welcome alternative to prostitution, child abandonment, and begging. Today, with increased divorce rates and more children born out of marriage, this aspect of Social Security overwhelmingly became welfare as we knew it (AFDC)—that is, before welfare reform. Means-tested, unpopular to both haves and have-nots, and enormously useful to the Right as a political football, welfare was the first element of Social Security to be axed. Meanwhile, as far as most people were aware, Social Security, or at least OASDI, remained the "third rail" of American politics (an urban expression referring to the high-voltage third rail of subway tracks). The melting of this third rail happened quickly, even for a country as dominated by corporations as we are.

Similar threats to policies like those of Social Security are occurring in other developed countries. These countries share with the United States what has come to be called "the graying of America"; yet, as shall become evident, the devastation of Social Security–type policy is not the only way to deal with old age. That developed countries are shredding their social policy in pursuit of consistency in free trade useful to corporations is a result of the corporate takeover of trade, as well as corporate control of other parts of the economy, the welfare state, and social policy. Further, the aging of baby boomers has established an important demographic truth. The number of baby boomers receiving Social Security payments when they retire will exceed the number of grown children paying into the system, which is only exacerbated by the reluctance of most baby boomers to have as many children as their parents had.

Medicine, already victorious in the treatment of infectious diseases in wealthy nations, turns not to doing something about infectious diseases in poor nations but rather to treating degenerative diseases that are the major cause of death in the developed world, such as cancer and heart disease, an effort profitable to insurance firms, pharmaceutical companies, and other corporations. This is particularly the case in America, which is prepared to pay some one-sixth of its wages to treat these diseases and thus lengthen the lives of its citizens. Thus not only do the boomers outnumber their children (never mind their grandchildren), but they also promise to live longer. Barring an unthinkable surge in immigration, a natural or an unnatural disaster, or social policy directed at shortening lives (to some extent an effect of managed care and the wish of some children to have their elderly relatives die with dignity, that is, sooner), the United States and the rest of the developed world are graying, balding, and whitening.

Social Security is a pact between generations and a credit to civil society. But significant discussion has begun to spread that it is a transfer program in which workers support nonworkers, in which mainly haves transfer monies mainly to have-nots. Indeed, a new class war is surfacing, not that between haves and have-nots but between young contributing workers and old parasitic golfers. Old folks drain medical care, day care, public schools, and other programs of monies that might otherwise be allocated to children. (No wonder the young poll as favoring physician-assisted suicide while the elderly are more likely to eschew the assistance.)

Whether to make Social Security a "pay as you go" or transfer system or a program that paid out only accrued benefits was an issue discussed at its beginnings. The conclusion was that it would be unjust to old people to make them beg, borrow, steal, or become paupers, so it was agreed to make it "pay as you go," while associating the program with notions of having worked for a lifetime and receiving only what one deserves, indeed what one is entitled to. Today, Social Security is increasingly spoken of neutrally as a transfer program, less neutrally as old people stealing from those who work; particularly when the old people are not *our* parents, they are even apt to be blamed for not having saved enough to fund their retirement.

The graying of America and the industrialized world is a demographic fact, which, like other demographic facts, could have been predicted. Perhaps its most severe consequences are in Japan since, in Japan, given this fact, people are inclined to save at the cost of spending and investing. Such behavior, rational for a population looking forward to its aging, is one reason for Japan's current economic state. Whether it also explains European economic weaknesses is more debatable. Until now, the macroeconomic consequences of aging have played differently on the American stage, contributing, however, to the growing gap between rich and poor.

Though the graying of America was in the demographic cards, certainly when the boomers had their children, only recently has it been proclaimed by the media and have its effects on corporate America been made visible. Meanwhile, a proliferation of drugstores awaits the arrival of senior citizens, golden oldies, and other euphemistically impaired people. Multiplex movie theaters are being made more comfortable and augmenting their youthful films with those that appeal to a more mature audience. Television programming is taking the elderly into account. No longer is the alternative medicine business restricted to the young (on whom it usually works because young people tend to get better anyway). Increasingly it is directed toward seniors. Old-age communities are no longer confined to the South, as corporate developers construct retirement housing and communities where old people need not encounter the young except, perhaps, as hired help, and young people need not be exposed to their future. In short, old age has become a growth industry. And this industry includes preparing financially for old age.

Whereas the wealthy have always prepared for old age, a gold mine has been discovered preparing middle-class haves for their retirement. The defined benefit pension, by which a worker is ensured a pension after retirement at some burden to the corporation, is being replaced by 401Ks, 403Bs, IRAs, and Roth IRAs (no relation to the author).

In lean and mean modern capitalism, the permanency of jobs decreases, responsibility and loyalty diminish, and the pension is increasingly an out-sourced business. One index is the vastly increased volume in the equity markets, desirable in a modern capitalist economy for corporations whose equities are bought and sold, for haves who have money to make on the market, and particularly for the financial services industry, already thriving so that Manhattan has undergone its own great transformation (i.e., high rents, low crime, a growth in wealth and income that more than makes up for the generally depressed conditions in the rest of New York State, a new culture industry, a growing art world, a tourist mecca, a policing laboratory, and so on; of course the happy old man from an older New York, spoken of earlier, would be arrested today for loitering).

The graying of America, a bona fide social fact, has been converted into a social problem, a media event, and has become part of the agenda of public policy. Not unexpectedly, the media coverage and policy discussion reflect the facts less than they do the interests of those involved in the discussion and a corporately controlled media. The most salient example of the urgency to "fix" this social problem is the talk of privatization of Social Security— that is, the transfer of economic enterprises, including social programs, in whole or in part, from the public sector to the private sector. Privatization is also a useful concept to apply to the diminution, evisceration, and elimination of public-sector programs where the functions of the public sector are picked up by the private sector, the not-for-profits, and informal networks, including families.

Current mythology has it that the private sector is more efficient, less bureaucratic, more responsive to people, speedier, more American, and more in keeping with globalization than the private sector. All these claims are questionable. In general, necessary links between privatization and markets are false, and links of privatization to globalization bear further investigation. To the extent that privatization is newspeak for corporatization, claims about civic responsibility, responsiveness to local needs, and so on are indeed false.

Linked to privatization in the American federal context is social policy's devolution to the states, which may then further devolve programs to counties and outsource them to the private and not-for-profit sectors. But federal power in have-not policies was instituted for good reason, as in the New Deal and in the attack on states' rights that was part of the civil rights movement. Devolution bears scrutiny. Claims that states know best, are less bureaucratic, and are closest to the problem than the federal government are questionable, particularly in this time of easy communication. Often devolution is newspeak for tax cuts, cuts in public programs, and capitulations to the corporate power that dominates state governments.

A dominant reference to privatization is that of the economies of the former Soviet bloc. According to the myth, in order for these once totalitarian Communist countries to become freedom-loving market economies, not only is privatization necessary but privatization of a recklessness matched only by that of the conversion of centralized economies into market economies. Such privatization and institution of free markets invites the assistance of corporate and academic contractors. Penetrated with a self-adulation of our superefficient lean and mean economy, the United State's model is spread throughout the world. The collapse of the Soviet Union raised such questions to the public agenda and in the corporate media. Attempts to privatize Social Security are poised to seem similar to the privatization sketched earlier.

In brief, the argument for the privatization of Social Security takes the following form: America is graying. Social Security is not an actuarially sound pension plan; it is a program that transfers money from workers to old people. When a sufficient number of baby boomers have retired, more claims will be made on the program than there will be FICA taxes going into it. Soon after, Social Security as we know it will become insolvent. Although 30 percent returns in the stock market may have been temporary, history shows average annual returns on the order of 10 percent, well above the returns paid by government instruments into which the remainder of Social Security taxes after paying current recipients are sent.

Further, we are told that more than money is at stake: the freedom to use our money as we wish. People should be allowed to invest in private instruments, not only because of the greater returns that will make up for future deficits, hence solving the crisis, but also because people have a right to decide how their own money is to be spent. (Indeed, this same reasoning applies to taxes, which are too high and, in any event, un-American, because they take freedom away from individuals to decide how they wish to spend their own resources.) The first slogan of the American Revolution was "no taxation without representation," something seemingly forgotten in this age of big and confiscatory government.

We take this to be a reasonably indulgent statement of claims to privatize Social Security. Of course, people differ in how much of it to privatize, exactly how to privatize, and about the role of federal regulation in any privatization. These important details, however, will not be undertaken here; rather, this discussion is restricted more modestly to the concept of privatization of Social Security itself. Even though the downturn in the stock market made Social Security seem suddenly a more solid and less foolish investment, it is still on President Bush's agenda. After all, Bush is unabashedly of, by, and for business, and business has much to gain from privatization. Arguably, the move to the right that this country enjoyed was only augmented by the high-tech new economy. In the media-hyped new version of democracy, corpocracy compatable, one dollar, one vote, replaced one person, one vote, as new generation X'ers became stock market activists.

The government sells bonds to the Social Security trust fund. No less conservative a figure than Alan Greenspan, Federal Reserve chairman, has observed that it makes no difference whether Social Security monies are destined for the government or corporations, for to the extent that they are not destined for the government, the government will have to seek money elsewhere. In so doing, interest rates or taxes are likely to be raised. In any case, Greenspan sees paying off the massive federal debt incurred during the excesses of the Reagan administration as the first priority. In his words, "It's a wash," private or public makes no difference. (After the president was selected by a power-hungry, activist, and partisan Supreme Court, and after a decent interval had passed, Chairman Greenspan became more obviously partisan and supported a tax cut, which will also make future reductions in spending for social policy necessary.)

If investment of Social Security in the private sector is no solution to the gap between monies coming in and flowing out, anticipated when baby boomers start withdrawing their Social Security, this does not seem to have stilled the voices, abated the discussion, or short-circuited the propaganda of the virtues of privatizing Social Security. Yet the real problem, according to Greenspan and most other economists, is investing in the present for the future. This would be greatly assisted by increased public and private savings rates, which is why Greenspan wanted to pay down the national debt, why he was leery of the wealth effect that makes people spend more as a result of increased capital gains on the equity markets, and why he favors technology and an educated labor force capable of using it—in short, all measures leading to economic growth. These sentiments remain even though some of the sudden wealth in our economy has disappeared. Most economists concur.

Although cynicism regarding Social Security is misplaced, it is only too well placed with regard to efforts to reform Social Security, to end Social Security as we know it, or to repeal Social Security. Indeed, the media is remarkable for its lack of critical comment, although the business press accurately reported Greenspan's criticisms. Of course, Greenspan is not the only critic of Social Security reform. Many others have voiced various complaints. Greenspan's critique is significant, however, because Greenspan is generally considered the most powerful man in the American economy, because the Federal Reserve system has served as a bastion for international capital markets, and because Greenspan attacks privatization in this country head on. The fate of Social Security reform remains to be seen, of course, given the numerous corporate interests with much to gain from its reform and privatization.

Best known as an entitlement to old people for a lifetime of hard work, and as a transfer payment, there is another interpretation of Social Security. Social Security is "insurance" against our old age, which was once a possibility but is now a probability. Social Security also insures against other market excesses. It insures young women from prostitution and old women from poverty in the event their working husbands die. This is only decent common sense. Of course the possibility that the wives of haves would also be protected assisted in this interpretation. The program also included children, without controversy for the same reasons. When the demographic facts changed and Aid to Dependent Children, later Aid to Families of Dependent Children, went largely to divorced women and their children and to unwed mothers and their children, this part of Social Security lost much of its constituency of haves, became referred to first as welfare, then welfare as we know it, and finally welfare as we knew it.

Over the years new programs were added—some means-tested, others not. Of the latter, perhaps the most significant was Medicare, now also under discussion for reform, including prescription drugs. Medicare for all—national health insurance—is important social policy that has never been passed in this country. Social Security Disability Insurance was a non-means-tested program directed toward those with a physical or health condition that prevented work. Like aid to widows, it could be interpreted as a right or a charity. With the overwhelming presence of disability-centered charities, it soon was viewed as charity. Supplemental Security Income, Food Stamps, WIC, Head Start, and other means-tested programs are stigmatized, under-funded, and fragmentary, as might be expected by programs seldom used by haves. Usually have-nots do not like these programs either, which is reason-able since the programs were designed and implemented by haves.

Today, a distinction is drawn between Social Security benefits for the elderly and what is referred to as the insurance parts of Social Security. One fear is that separating the pension part of Social Security from the insurance part will fix the pension part while diminishing support for the insurance part, which is currently paid largely from Social Security taxes. Preferable is to regard all or no Social Security programs as insurance and to acknowledge that the major division is between haves and have-nots.

Closely related to what have-nots may perceive as a divide-and-conquer strategy among haves is Social Security reform, particularly privatization. Social Security is not only an economic issue, but a social and political issue as well. Social Security is an entitlement. Reform threatens to remove its status as an entitlement for all and instead to consider it a privilege. Reform also threatens the intergenerational contract, transforming it into a conflict between have-nots and haves under the guise of a conflict between the working young and the nonworking old. Given the strength of corporate interests, the tone of prior rhetoric, and the instincts of the Bush adminis-tration, even though current proposals are for only partial privatization of Social Security, this is most prudently and realistically regarded as a foot in the door. A major triumph of Social Security has been to ensure a com-munity of expectation and an absence of conflict among its recipients and among working have-nots. Social Security reform jeopardizes this guarantee if it takes on the character of privatization. In that case, it will be every man, woman, and child for him- or herself.

It is tragic that a genuine demographic fact should be the occasion of Social Security reform in the same sense that there was welfare reform — that is, not reform but repeal. Repeal of Social Security would be as justified by the facts as was the repeal of welfare. The challenge in the case of Social Security is not to undo something that has already been done; indeed, the challenge is to preserve Social Security, the centerpiece of our welfare state, to reform it in ways that keep it alive. Social Security not only is central to our welfare state, but is one of its most popular creations. This challenge can be met, particularly if it is addressed before the elements of Social Security having to do with the have-nots are separated from those having to do with haves.

Some simple modifications to Social Security are offered here only as examples that would be sufficient to save Social Security as we know it, to keep the program as it is. Do not privatize all or part of it. Do not separate the old-age parts from the insurance parts. Do not use the graying of America as a flashpoint for intergenerational conflict. Further, remove the caps on the FICA taxes. It is important to remove rather than raise these caps partially because of inflation, which will put more people above the cap, partially because the wealthy can afford to pay, and because removing the cap is a straightforward way to have an effect on the income disparity between haves and have-nots.

Tax Social Security benefits under the same provisions that govern the taxation of earned and unearned income while paying into Social Security. Remove the current fixed rates of taxation on some Social Security benefits. Continue taxing after a person reaches seventy. Provide a significant tax credit, like the Earned Income Tax Credit, for all Social Security recipients, which tax credit should be set at a level high enough to offset any harm to poor people from taxing Social Security benefits. The Internal Revenue Service is as reasonable a way to collect monies from the old as from the young, and allowing for taxation to kick in gradually has the benefit of not discouraging work. There is no reason except sentimental guilt for removing tax liabilities at age seventy.

A person at sixty-five (or sixty-seven) is less likely to be frail, burned out, or sickly than was once the case. The older the age of eligibility for Social Security benefits, the less expensive the program. One proposal suggests raising the eligibility age. Not unreasonably, some have taken issue with this, arguing that people in some jobs are far more likely to need Social Security earlier than those in other jobs. Unfortunately, it will not do to suggest that OSHA be strengthened, that certain jobs be designated as hazardous enough to require private pensions, or that the nature of work be changed. Although all these are reasonable and would constitute partial solutions to the age limit, the current application of them in this context is inappropriate because there is already a wide constituency in favor of keeping Social Security more or less as we know it, while constituencies for these other alterations are now weaker. However, vigorous enforcement of and, where appropriate, legislation regarding the prohibition of involuntary termination of employment for reasons of age should be in place (i.e., firing for reasons of age should be prohibited, and prohibition must be enforced). Thus early retirement should not be forced, but retiring later ought not be discouraged.

Medicare must accompany Social Security, because old people are more likely to need medical care, and they are less apt to be able to afford it. (More on this later.) Further, in no event should the graying of America be an excuse for the impoverishment of many old people. Nor need it be. The most visible and venal repeal of Social Security as we know it would occur by separating the insurance and pension aspects of the program, leaving the former to the government. The political pressure to do just this is great. In the short term, before interest rates are raised, privatization will benefit the corporate sector. In both the short and the long term, privatization will benefit that part of the corporate sector concerned with financial assets, the mutual fund industry, stock brokers, the Internet, and insurance companies. In 1999 Congress, under enormous pressure from financial interests, broke down the wall erected during the New Deal between the savings and loan function of traditional banks and the handling of insurance and many other financial instruments (like equities), making the already powerful financial corporations even more powerful and profitable. The financial sector has already benefited from government subsidies (through tax benefits) like IRAs, 401Ks, and 403Bs, which have already added to the volume of financial transactions.

Private investment will not pay for public goods, like public education, which is ever more necessary as our technology becomes more complex. Certain government outlays—for education, job training, and infrastructure, for example—are not expenditures but investments, the encouragement of which will help increase the productivity of our economy to help pay for retired baby boomers. The graying of America is soluble by judicious investments that increase productivity. Given the current underinvestment in have-nots, this might be a good place to start. Put another way, the division between the generations is a translation of the division between haves and have-nots. Given this, privatization of all or part of Social Security and other forms of Social Security repeal, inaugurated in welfare reform, only increase the distance between haves and have-nots.

Currently Social Security is under assault in the United States. Attacks on variants of it under various names like pension reform lag in Europe where a progressive Third Way, tuned to changing requirements of global bureaucratic capitalism, has taken the baton from an earlier period of

Reaganism–Thatcherism. (In countries like Chile there is no need for re-form, "reform" having been anticipated by a government constructed in the shadow of transnational corporations and U.S. dominance.)

In the United States, the attack on Social Security proceeds, public re-lations describing it as a necessary solution to the graying of America, as an equal chance for all to make money on the stock market (although this has become less attractive with the market downturn that seemingly appeared from nowhere between the 2000 presidential election and the inauguration of the younger President Bush), and as greater freedom for individuals to spend their money however they want to. However, given the number of Americans in favor of the welfare state, it is to be expected that the most successful attacks on Social Security are made by wolves lurking in sheep's clothing. They bleat about the graying of America, about the need for us to be competitive in a global economy, and about the virtues of personal re-sponsibility in providing for our own future. Until now, the wolf is alive and well.

# 7   Health

Although everyone wants it, health is difficult to define. Most hold it as something more than the absence of disease. The United States spends some 16 percent of its gross domestic product attempting to achieve it. There are various proxies for it—for example, life expectancy and infant mortality rate. The location of disease within our bodies is surprisingly new[1] and the discovery of causes for diseases even newer. Newest of all is the ability to do something about disease, even to cure it.

George Washington was not killed by his serious infectious disease but by the heroic therapy he received: bleeding. If Stalin had to be a bit imprudent to fear doctors, Rousseau's injunction to avoid them was, at least in retrospect, altogether sane. With the human genome project ahead of schedule,[2] medicine has forged a pact of critical importance, first with careful systematic observation, and later, increasingly, with science. All this is to say that medicine has changed, is currently changing, and will change in the future. At least for now and in the future, we can substitute the word "progress" for "change."

Yet medical progress and social change diverge. Barring significant changes in society, they will diverge further. If social change increasingly tilts society toward the benefits of haves, the divergence between medical and social change will not be to the benefit of have-nots. The patterns exist today, with whites living almost a decade longer than African-Americans, the United States being a world mecca for the best medicine for the rich, some 45 million people in the United States uninsured, the poor areas being poorly served, developing nations plagued by diseases long banished from developed nations, and so on.

If we spend 16 percent of the GDP for health care, few of us behave as if we believe health is that important. For example, our lives are likely to be too sedentary, with sporadic, even isometric, exercise. We use too many drugs too often, including sugar, nicotine, alcohol. Our diets have too much fat (the use of fats in fast foods fattens not only us, but the profits of corporations).

Many of us are couch potatoes, a complicated result of stay-at-home lives, a lack of civic society, and electronic progress (increasingly digital) that will soon replace even today's entertainment centers by wide-screen, high-resolution, high-band-width, interactive, multi-channel, multi-use home environments where many of us will be couch potatoes even as we work and consume at home. (This page was written at home, but in a swivel chair — not on a couch.) The production of home entertainment environments will be even more profitable for corporations than the production of entertainment centers, never mind the lone television set.

A book about our unhealthy "lifestyles" (newspeak for the articulation of our lives with corporate production, consumption, and profit) is hardly necessary, there already being innumerable books and other forms of entertainment that articulate, propagandize, and provide images of our current lifestyle, a word announcing to corporations malleability, fit, and change; in the words written for General Electric, even before it acquired NBC, "Progress is our most important product." Of course, this is less true in have-not countries, where corporations often pollute, exploit, and otherwise degrade the lives of citizens.

Here, the aim is merely to observe that most of us want health but do not behave in ways that foster health. This, of course, is a contradictory paradox in the lifestyle we lead, which increases the profits of powerful corporations. We are a generation that has forgotten the virtue of hand washing while demanding that physicians treat us with antibiotics for maladies we might have prevented. We are likely to shower daily and medicate our overly dry skin. We eat fast foods while praising coronary bypass surgery. Such behavior contradicts our desire for health; moreover, it greatly increases both the demand for medical services and the profits corporations reap from, say, fast foods and the technologies associated with bypass surgery. In fact, most discussions of health care are discourses on medical services. Much modern talk of health care regards it as a commodity. Problems discussed have to do with the use, organization, and delivery of this commodity.

But surely it is a strange commodity; few of us are even sure when we need to contact a "physician" (a word I shall use interchangeably with the longer locution "health care system").

Usually we see a physician only if we feel sick. The word "feel" is important here. Some of us may be more inclined than others to ride out a cold by gulping down our mother's chicken soup. *Feeling* sick is subjective. Indeed, many of us may be reluctant to see a physician even when we feel sick, sometimes for economic reasons. Others may see a physician to rule out disease. Still others may see a physician for reassurance, for amateur "shrinking," or for a note to get out of work or school. Some estimates are that some half of the visits to a primary-care physician are medically unnecessary. Surely this accounts in part for the increasing use of alternative medicine, chiropractors, unorthodox therapists, even teenagers working in health food stores, who are likely to be better trained in sales (appearing congenial, pleasant, and courteous) than in health care. Yet certain diseases are likely to be ignored, like cancer, atherosclerosis, and diabetes, whose early symptoms require a physician not only for diagnosis and treatment, but frequently for initial recognition.

The physician may order tests, perhaps partly fearing a malpractice suit. The patient does not order the tests. If a specialist is required, the primary-care physician says so and may even recommend the specialist. In short, patients have little say about their medical care. Although medical care is ostensibly reckoned a market commodity, according to economic theory it must be a most curious commodity because consumer choice is not only irrational and uninformed, but often relinquished to physicians. All this, and more, make the patient a curious consumer. For example, most of us purchase health care less informed about its quality than we are about the quality of hats we buy. To the extent that information is lacking, the vaunted freedom to choose one's physician is besides the point. Were patients fully informed, everyone would try to see the best physicians. There would be hoards at their doors, and, in a free market, they would charge considerably more than physicians with lesser qualifications. Some such market behavior occurs, but more often physicians are chosen according to whether they have a medical degree, are pleasant, and are conveniently located. Health Maintenance Organizations (HMOs) can commission arguably spurious qualities in the medical care that they market, employing tour guides to show how well the HMO meets the prospective patients' desires and expectations. (In New York State, even interior decorators who design their waiting rooms are likely to be licensed.) HMOs, managed care, and corporations represent health care in fashions familiar to us from other marketing mechanisms. Of course, ultimately it is not we the patients (mere commodities) to whom health care is marketed but rather the private insurance corporations or the government, the real consumers.

Thus two sorts of marketing take place—one directed to us, and the other to the real consumers, which are increasingly insurance companies and the government. We are important insofar as the health care institutions can expand in terms of the number of people covered and then sell this coverage to other corporations. The ultimate sale to the genuine consumer is not made with the familiar hyper-commercialization. Instead, it resembles market transactions between corporations or between corporations and the government. The advertising involved differs, as is evident from the trade publications. Here, as in much of our lives, we do not even enjoy market freedom, the freedom that was to have been reserved to people as consumers increasingly being turned over to other corporations.

In one of his jewel-like essays, Lewis Thomas brilliantly compares the medical experience of Joe Patient with that of a member of the family of an internist, who is the primary-care physician for her family, knows which specialists may be needed, and can make an informed judgment that medical care is warranted.[3] There was once a saying that the shoemakers' family's shoes were often in disrepair. When medical care was ostensibly a market commodity, the internist's family usually received different and better medical care. Indeed, were it not the case that physicians exchanged free services, only physicians' families (and the rich and powerful, who could tap into networks of information, and who were friendly with physicians) could buy health care as a commodity about which they had appropriate information and freedom of choice, at a time when medicine was cheaper. For most Americans in the old days, medicine was a curious market commodity.[4]

Still, health care was portrayed as a market commodity. For example, the American Medical Association (AMA) protested Medicare as a socialist betrayal of free-market capitalist health care. But medical care had ceased to qualify as a genuine free-market commodity, and the AMA was merely protecting the privilege of its members. The AMA's premonitions about bureaucratic socialized health care were to be partially realized without socialism. Medicare, Medicaid, and private insurance increased dramatically, and third-party payment made health care accessible to vastly more people. The buyer or patient had no economic incentive to reduce expenses, and physicians had no economic incentive to control costs. There still was a buyer, but the buyer was a third party like an insurance company or the government. Whereas traditionally the patient had sort of looked like the buyer and the physician the seller, this illusion is inapplicable in modern medicine.

Substantial progress in medical care was achieved in the decades after Medicare was established. Our number-one killer is still heart disease, but in the past three decades cardiology has progressed to include open-heart surgery, safe and effective coronary bypass surgery, angioplasty, stents, angiograms, classes of effective medications for hypertension, and so on. The completion of the comprehensive Framingham study statistically isolated cardiac risk factors such as smoking, high cholesterol, family history, and age. In short, cardiology (and almost every medical specialty) can do incomparably more now than when Medicare was first passed.

Thus progress has made medicine more valuable. Further, even when adjusted for inflation, medical care has become more expensive. The effectiveness of medicine has contributed to increased life spans, contributing to the graying of America, which only adds to the increasing demand for medicine (old people need more of the increasingly expensive product). Consequently, medicine boomed, health care costs zoomed, and regulations and organizational change by third-party payers loomed.

It is not true that today payers have no choice, that they have no say in medical decision making, or that medicine is less a market commodity than it once was. Quite the contrary. The fact is simply that patients no longer substantially pay the bills; thus they have no voice except that given them by managed-care conglomerates, insurance companies, and the government, which are overwhelmingly the new paying consumers of health care. All three have an interest in decreasing expenses, the first two to increase profits, and the third to avoid tax increases. Occasionally this breaks into the news with stories on the "medical bill of rights," drive-through mastectomies, the withholding of heroic procedures, and physician-assisted suicide, all of which affect the cost of health care, including that for haves.

At one time, physicians were archetypical professionals. Today, they are likely to work for HMOs, hospitals, medical schools, or insurance companies—in short, for corporations. While the cost of medicine has skyrocketed (as have the profits of insurance companies, drug companies, and the makers of medical hardware), the money, which increasingly looks like salaries in corporations other than those concerned with health, has decreased in real dollars for general and family practitioners, psychiatrists, and pediatricians. Most often, only specialists have maintained their salaries, and only super-specialists have increased them. Most physicians are subject to work speed-ups, salary negotiations, and unwanted supervision, all once in the realm of factory workers. The corporations that employ them are powerful, profitable, market themselves, and even have sufficient perks to attract business students who, once upon a time, might have gone into medicine. Health care is not only a business, but is a big corporate business with important profits.

Medical care today differs markedly from that which was available to President Washington. Most significant is that today's medicine delivers. It cures or prevents most infectious diseases. Perhaps the most remarkable feature of the human immunodeficiency virus (HIV) is that it is an infectious disease that can be neither cured nor prevented by a simple vaccination. One may often forget that syphilis, now curable, was also a sexually transmitted disease of enormous social consequence. The iron lungs of our parents' generation have been replaced by routine vaccinations. At one time, the side effects of tuberculosis included an investment in the Adirondack Mountains tourist trade in the form of sanitariums and the legendary Doc Holiday, tubercular sidekick of Wyatt Earp. Further, infectious diseases contributed in a major way to the initial formation of American suburbs, as the wealthy moved from the "unhealthy" cities, frequently overcrowded with immigrants, to the clean air of the suburbs. Today, tuberculosis has receded under the assault of antibiotics and better plumbing. Indeed, so successful has been the elimination of infectious diseases that they are now largely forgotten, with the exception of AIDS, which tore, unexpected and unwelcome, into our social fabric.

At one time, heart disease was largely a consequence of infection. Today, heart infections are rare and usually treatable. More significant, infectious chains like strep throat leading to rheumatic fever leading to endocarditis are usually stopped at the gate, by treating the strep infection with antibiotics before complications set in. In short, modern medicine has conquered the bugs. The Darwinian evolution of drug-resistant strains has, until now, been held in check by ever newer, more expensive, and more profitable antibiotics. Whether this trend will continue in the future or whether the bugs will win is an important question.

Not only has medicine delivered on infectious diseases, but it has ameliorated an assortment of other diseases as well. Biotechnology, psychopharmacology, and the sequencing of the human genome promise much more in the near future. But even today, medicine is extraordinarily effective. One might plausibly argue that today's high cost of medicine is well worth it. Since medicine can save lives, and since life, of course, is a given if one is to enjoy all the other economic goods and services, ought we not be only too happy to pay for it? Put differently, although the cost of medicine has outpaced the cost of most other services today, is it not the case that what is bought today is not the same good as was bought in the past?

Today's medicine differs not only in what it can deliver, but in its bureaucratic organization and in its relationship to patients, to health care workers, and to corporations. In medicine, as in many other areas of high technology, the government subsidizes much research. For example, the government funds basic research in biomedicine (it was not only by government funding but in government agencies that the human genome project first took off). Government subsidizes teaching hospitals affiliated with universities. University teaching hospitals grew enormously in the last decades, and they now account for about half the nonscience-related revenues at many universities. Cuts in Medicaid and Medicare not only threaten have-nots, but also plague teaching hospitals, the scientific and clinical research that takes place there, and universities in general. In short, much of the current and future infrastructure of modern medicine is threatened by cuts in Medicare and Medicaid. Medicare and Medicaid are programs not simply for have-nots, but also for modern corporate medical capitalism. In some measure, it is this that has made them difficult to slash, and cutting them may be achievable only by means of refined laser surgery.

Is it not rational to spend so much for medicine? To the extent that it is, is the much-discussed health care crisis a problem or an opportunity? Few argue that we pay too much for education, food, and clothes, while some argue that we do not pay enough for clean air, pure water, or fighting aesthetic pollution. The irrationality of medical expenditures, in newspeak health care costs, is not self-evident. Indeed, high medical costs may offer an increasingly powerful corporate sector pretext for change that is profitable to corporations and to the benefit of haves, as does the Social Security crisis, the end of welfare as we knew it, and so on.

In the words of Judith Feder and Marilyn Moon:

The enactment of Medicare in 1965 reflected political support for three fundamental principles regarding health care for the elderly. We decided then that insurance is the right way to spread the risk to the elderly of sizable health care costs, that redistributing income through the tax system is necessary to make that insurance affordable and universal, and that the insurance and taxes are best administered by the federal government if the system is to serve all of the elderly regardless of their income or health. These principles of insurance, redistribution, and government responsibility are now at risk. The challenge comes from both sides of the political aisle in proposals that would convert Medicare from a universal entitlement to public insurance into a government voucher for private insurance.[5]

By substituting the phrase "at risk" with "under assault," this statement seems to make complete sense. Yet the current attacks use the rising costs of Medicare as an excuse for the substitution of suggested programs like medical savings accounts and vouchers that would allow free choice in health care, meaningful only to haves with the proper connections and to relatively healthy people who not only can choose but be chosen by private health care plans that can increase their profits by serving haves and the healthy (the two are connected). Under attack is health insurance, the costs born by all (haves included), the benefits in principle going to all (both haves and have-nots), and substitution by a system that further increases the distance between haves and have-nots during their ages of eligibility even beyond that difference ensured by the longer lives of haves than have-nots.

Other effects of the attack are much like the approaching assault on Social Security and the successful attack on welfare as we knew it. In fact, it is not questions of distribution, free choice, or even price that follow logically, but questions about the percentage of our GDP that should properly be applied to health care. Such matters are discussed more rarely, of course, since they have less obvious benefits for haves, nor do they profit insurance companies and other large corporations in the health care industry.

The economic issues in medicine include efficiency and equity. The organizational issues include access, organization (increasingly modeled after business), payment, rationing, expensive technologies, public image and HMOs, managed care, preferred provider networks, and bureaucracy. The business issues include profit maximization, mergers, patent agreements, strategic alliances, dealing with products that change, and administering nursing and medical education (which are labor intensive). Let us first turn to the social and political issues.

The AMA was correct in recognizing that Medicare and Medicaid threatened its well-being and that of its members, although not for reasons of socialism or for the protection of some perfect free market in medical care that never existed. Medicare, Medicaid, and private insurance are funded by taxes or employers, which generally, it is conceded, pass on the costs to employees in the form of decreased salaries. In any event, taxes are not paid on most medical insurance premiums, and hence tax expenditures are extracted from the government to pay for employer-based insurance. With the increase of third-party payments, medicine temporarily lost any pretense of being a reasonable market commodity, there being no market disincentive for physicians to charge more, to perform unnecessary tests, or to order proliferating medical procedures. Further, patients had no reason to decline such procedures and tests; moreover, in many patients' minds, high costs even came to define good medicine. After all, the patient was not paying, and the physician was being reimbursed by a distant third party. Thus costs to third-party payers escalated. Third parties, notably starting with the government, issued regulations, fixed and lowered reimbursement schedules, and paid hospitals not per day but according to procedure. Insurance companies followed suit. Such regulation is expensive and bureaucratic. Important medical decisions were made by a faceless voice at the other end of a telephone. Initially, physicians were besieged with paper work. Subsequently, many banded together in groups and hired office managers.

The bond between physician and patient loosened, along with the patient's faith and trust in the physician. (Why did this trust exist in the first place? It may be explained in part by economics, that physicians relied on patients for their livelihood. But surely such trust transcends economics. Some physicians believe that it arose from the "laying on of hands," an element of the earlier physical examination. Psychologically, the physician was often the substitute for an all-wise parent. Existentially, it came from the belief that physicians provide health and, *in extremis*, even life.)

Today, however, medicine is called health care and is delivered through Health Maintenance Organizations, Preferred Provider Networks, hospitals, and other intermediaries. At one time, most such organizations were not-for-profit. However, to facilitate the raising of capital, to enhance mergers, to articulate better with corporations that operate for profit, health care organizations that were once not-for-profit are converting. In addition, for-profit health care organizations spin off from insurance companies and other for-profit corporations. Like other for-profit corporations, their proclaimed goal is to maximize profits. This occurs in traditional corporate fashion by increasing efficiency, decreasing expenses, increasing prices, rationalizing procedures, substituting nurses and physician assistants for physicians, developing incentives to save, and initiating regulations to preclude the use of expensive medications, procedures, tests, specialists, and super-specialists, and so on. (For example, some 20 percent of the studies done on Aricept, a drug for "commodities" with Alzheimer's, usually elderly "commodities," published during the year 2000, dealt with whether use of the drug would be "cost effective,"[6] newspeak for "profitable.")

In such organizations, physicians are simply employees, usually with stipulated time to spend with each patient. Newer, expensive drugs are often passed over for older, generic drugs. The insurance company or another third party is a wary customer with an interest in minimizing outlays per patient. Thus the relationship between provider and customer is more like a market relationship than once was true between physician and patient. The patient has little say. Expanding providers increase their number of patients by negotiating with corporations, enhancing public relations, and advertising. Market share is expanded by increasing the number of payers, partially patients and small companies but more typically corporations and government. The patient is just another factor of production, a commodity, a case, a number. Indeed, we have come a long way from the former doctor–patient relationship as we enter the brave new world of health care organization as a corporation.

Many physicians and patients are uncomfortable with current medical care. Both may complain that medicine has ceased to be human, compassionate, and patient-friendly. Indeed, many patients are put off by health care organizations because they are impatient, impersonal, and hurried. Patients enter health care organizations somewhat like travelers entering an airport in this lean-and-mean age of corporate deregulation. If medicine at one time was irrational, today it has been rationalized.

Modern health care has led to the expansion of a new form of applied corporate ethics. Like legal ethics, corporate ethics, and social work ethics, medical ethics has flourished. For example, many hospitals may have ethical review panels, and medical schools coursework in medical ethics. Sometimes medical ethics is applied to a particular case, sometimes it deals with the ethical implications of medical change, but almost always medical ethics furnishes impartial judgment, such impartiality often reinforced by being outsourced to think tanks, foundations, universities, or businesses that specialize in making ethical choices. Like other branches of corporate ethics, medical ethics makes impossible situations possible, renders "impartial" verdicts in contested cases, and, indeed, is intrinsic to the system of public relations so indispensable to modern corporations. Like the Better Business Bureau and movie ratings, self-regulation is preferable to government legislation. At the very least, corporate ethics in all forms serves to justify corporate conduct (even when an impartial ethical decision disagrees with corporate practice, for corporate ethics is as impartial as the modern press). In short, corporate ethics constitutes a receptacle in which a small but troublesome portion of the corporate buck stops.

For example, a political situation at Texaco was outsourced to an ethics company. It is not surprising that corporate ethics would justify corporate conduct. Experts on medical ethics are well-paid witnesses in lawsuits and appear before organs of social policy. Academic medical ethics renders significant concrete human experience into abstraction confronted not in human terms but academically. Consider Nazi Germany, where the murder of mentally ill, retarded, and disabled people[7] went forward under an ethical mandate that was an empowered state-endorsed version of eugenics, a long-forgotten element of American progressivism. The extension of this mandate to Jews, gypsies, and homosexuals was by way of interpreting these people as wounds, cancers, and syphilitic grotesqueries on the Nazi *Volk* (very roughly, "body politic").

Although there are certainly extreme problems with a "therapeutic state," the use of medicine by a powerful regime, medicine's role in the welfare state as a controlling mechanism, even questions of euthanasia and genocide, and so on, we shall only touch on these issues. Medical marginalization and professionalism can, however, constitute a regime of power that extends well beyond the boundaries of health. A therapeutic state that includes the medicalization of the social, the tyranny of the medical model, the craft and cruelty of professionalism, and the power of medical labeling, diagnosis, and marginalization[8] is becoming largely of historical interest. If not today, then in the near future these matters will be consumed by the cold fires of power, money, and corporate domination. Here, on a more modest note, we question certain features of modern medicine that have changed with organized corporate health care.

Modern medicine may be sufficiently efficacious so as to warrant the expenditure of a large part of our GDP. This is not to say, of course, that modern medicine can cure everything, nor should it be an invitation to take up a gluttonous, sedentary, or otherwise unhealthy lives. Physicians are neither infallible nor invulnerable to financial influence; as an example, they often learn about new drugs from advertisements or studies financed by pharmaceutical corporations. Our media are saturated with, say, successful anticancer experiments in mice that proclaim forthcoming cures. Not all medical procedures are called for, never mind successful, but to deny advances in medical research is not a matter of skepticism but is outright foolishness.

Given valuable modern medicine that promises to become ever more valuable in the future, what is a reasonable relationship between such medicine and the citizens of our country? Medicine's engagement with science changes medical practice ever more rapidly; thus the answer to this question is not static. The essential questions include how medicine should be organized, who should pay for it and how much, and how it should be rationed and distributed. Considering only its costs, the delivery of "health care" should be efficient. But it is currently inefficient, and the future promises only more inefficiency. One culprit, the administrative bureaucracy that so burdens modern health care, could be streamlined with a single third-party payer, something resembling that which exists in Canada.[9] Arbitrary and powerful quantifications of a different sort than the market have a growing place in medicine. Whether such quantifications should hold such a position is not obvious, however. A classic example is the question of what a human life is worth. The current organization of health care delivery is often disagreeable, as is true of much corporate organization in general. The arguments for making corporate organization in health care delivery more democratic are essentially the same as for other corporations.

Like any scarce resource, health care is rationed, once by a fee for services where the payer was the patient. This form of rationing is of antiquarian interest. Today, rationing is by third-party payers. Some 45 million Americans are uninsured, thereby making of them second-class citizens of health care. This state of affairs, although tolerable to those who are insured, is abominable to most without insurance. Thus the primary requirement of a just health care system is that all be insured, which is consistent with a single-payer plan. Haves tend to be more healthy than have-nots—an observation available to common sense and social science. Haves are more likely to be insured and to have better insurance than have-nots. Information regarding optimal medical care is likely to be more accessible to haves. Here, as so often, have-nots include disproportionately more African-Americans, Latinos, immigrants, disabled people, women, and the elderly.

The late King Hussein of Jordan flew his own private jet to the Mayo

Clinic for the "best care money could buy." Even a commoner like Larry King hired a MedEvac jet for the trip from Los Angeles to New York Hospital, where he had confidence in the physician performing an angioplasty on the day of King's wedding. Even haves who are not celebrities or do not qualify for a luxurious corner suite in a major metropolitan hospital are far more likely to sample the best of America's medicine, while Medicaid patients may not see attending physicians but rather interns and residents in the same hospitals. Such inequality in medical care may be regarded in three ways: (1) as just another example of inequality in our country, (2) as an indication that health care has an obligation to aspire to equality, and (3) as evidence that health care is exempt from obligations to equality. (Do you really begrudge the president the very best in medical care?)

Another aspect of rationing is stimulated by third-party payers that have an economic interest in paying as little as possible and are powerful enough to issue regulations or to organize contracts. "Drive-through mastectomies" and "overnight deliveries" have became notorious since haves have been the victims. HMOs ration the use of specialists, medical tests, drugs, and time. They increasingly "cream" the healthy and the affluent who need less medical care, leaving third-rate medicine to have-nots, who generally require more.

Many diseases may be prevented by simple and inexpensive means—for example, vaccines, adequate plumbing, healthy foods, and moderate exercise.[10] But curing these same diseases may be expensive, difficult, and prolonged. A rationing system like ours, which allocates too little for prevention in favor of cure, is perverse. Preventive measures, too, are aberrant: evil is pathologized into mental illness, infectious and quasi-infectious diseases are "treated" by some form of quarantine (e.g., urban ghettos, jails, and hospitals), the "good life" is replaced by "quality of life," crime is defined as a disease, addiction is treated as a crime, disability is considered an incurable disease, and hygiene ranges from hand washing to euthanasia. Such a therapeutic state is an impenetrable barrier to democracy.[11]

Yet selective, appropriate, or isolated measures of prevention need not eventuate in the kind of therapeutic state alluded to earlier. These include vaccination programs; prenatal, neonatal, and child care; high schools where overweight adolescents are occupied with playful activity; prohibitions against tobacco companies hooking teenagers on nicotine; recognition by colleges that binge drinking is dangerous; and increased information on nutrition.

In poor countries, corporations are likely to be aggressive in the marketing of cigarettes, baby formula, and other harmful products and practices while taking little interest in the development or promotion of inexpensive, unprofitable vaccines. Indeed, such corporate activity exists among have-nots in our own country. Corporate dominance, both at home and abroad, must be challenged by civic power. More funds should flow to the World Health Organization, to have-not nations, to nongovernmental organizations (NGOs), as well as to public health programs and health education for less-advantaged Americans.

Changes in medical technologies are unpredictable. Hence, amending Medicare, never mind designing new health care systems, is more complex than amending Social Security. Yet similarities exist, such as the appearance of crises in Medicare (e.g., coverage for prescription drugs), Social Security, and welfare. Although these problems are significant, their elevation to crisis proportions is a result of the media's manipulation of corporate propaganda, which propose, or have proposed, the increased rationalization, privatization, and creation of profitable domains for corporate cultivation.

At its maximum, health care means the difference between life and death. Virtually everyone prefers the former. Economically speaking, life is a prerequisite for the advancement of all happiness. This enhances the urgency of medical issues, the popularity of medicine in the media, and the importance patients attach to medical care. For all these reasons, a national health service, perhaps in a meaningful market, perhaps socialized, such as are Veterans Administration hospitals, is preferable. In any event, payment should be by a single third-party payer, free from corporate pressure. Rationing must be democratically discussed, with real protection for those who are old, vulnerable, disabled, or otherwise stigmatized and marginalized.

In the era of contagion, haves had an interest in the health of have-nots. Submerged in a sea of have-nots, haves could escape infectious disease only if have-nots remained healthy and lived in sanitary conditions, with vermin and other vectors held in check. The current concern among haves regarding AIDS is illustrative of this. However, when disease is not infectious, such as heart disease, cancer, diabetes, and asthma, the difference between public health and private health looms large. In such cases, haves are able virtually to ignore the health of have-nots, especially when the latter are isolated in a ghetto or in a distant nation.

The health care of haves welcomes the growing influence of insurance companies, pharmaceutical companies, and the home-entertainment industry. Whereas once health care was too scattered, diffuse, and even disreputable even to be considered a system, today it is openly declared an industry.[12] Much of its present state and its future is shared with other industries in America, where corporations have been downsized, computerized, divested, and merged. One consequence of these developments is the increasing power of the corporate sector, which, nonetheless, as political economist Charles E. Lindblom observes, is pluralistic in its decision making, for there are many corporations.[13]

Corporations share an interest in growth, profit, opening international markets (even as some wish to protect domestic markets from international competition), trade, and a healthy and flexible labor force. It is significant that workers' benefits are a liability to corporations. This is of particular interest in health care, because a time may arrive when many corporations will prefer that health care be universal to ensure employee flexibility (if underfunded, of course, and controlled by insurance corporations).

The health care sector has risen in value disproportionately to most other sectors. Planned obsolescence is no fad, the technologies of today often outstripping the technologies of yesterday. Not-for-profit HMOs, once supported by taxpayers, are becoming for-profit organizations in search of greater capital for mergers and expansion (this is true even of Blue Cross). Drug companies have designs on specialties. For example, some cancer centers have already developed relationships with pharmaceutical companies that plan to replace them. Corporate influence holds with research as well. For example, the experimental drugs Angiostatin and Endostatin were developed by a team at a hospital connected with the Harvard Medical School and the corporation Entremed. Stocks for Entremed rose with the announcement of these drugs' efficacy against cancers in mice.

The government helps support medical education, partially through Medicaid and Medicare, partially through low-interest loans, and partially by research, including that conducted by the National Institutes of Health and the Department of Energy (adapting to a contemporary post–cold war world in which nuclear weapons are less of a priority), spearheading a transformation of biology culminating in the sequencing of the human genome,[14] basic research of immense interest to biotechnology companies, pharmaceutical companies, agri-business, waste disposal, and sectors of the economy yet to be developed. All these corporate endeavors profit from socialized research paid for by taxpayers, who then pay for it once again as patients.

This is a sketchy map of a domain influenced by organizational theory, tax policy, transnational corporations, intellectual property, trade policy, and policies of all federal departments from Commerce to Energy to Defense. The corporate sector and the public sector work together. Increasingly, the public sector is dominated not by people but by corporations, which, in a Supreme Court decision, were given the rights of persons under the Fourteenth Amendment. As a member of Eisenhower's cabinet, Charles Wilson, observed, "What's good for General Motors is good for the country," words echoing those of President Coolidge when he announced that "the business of America is business."

Such corporate engulfment of democracy is abhorrent. The question here, however, is whether such corporate domination is beneficial or detrimental to health care. Any consumer of the nightly news is informed of advances in medicine, of the pathos of people in Third World countries, often children, who are victims of diarrhea, starvation, measles, and other horrors virtually banished from America. Investments in the human genome project will have a high payoff. (The program was initially sold to Congress as the best way to fight cancer, a sales pitch that may turn out to be true.)

Of course, claims the media, some inequality of health care may indeed result from the American system of corporate medicine, but surely the corporate tide will raise all boats, surely the benefits of corporate medicine will trickle down to have-nots. Messages from the media percolate down through our culture: for example, life is tough; human nature is greedy; you can't change things; don't rock the boat; be cynical; be apathetic; attend to your own private life and your own family values; be responsible for your own choices; take care of yourself; you are your most valuable possession; be charitable to those less fortunate than you for that will make you feel good. Realizing and accepting that there is a world beyond the self, beyond the media, and beyond the wisdom of pundits is difficult—as is recognizing the need for freedom, equality, and democracy.

As for rationing, health care is already rationed: once by the ability to pay for it and now, more usually, by having adequate insurance. The injustice of the differences in income and wealth between haves and have-nots has been discussed. This same injustice extends to health care. But because the enjoyment of other benefits and resources may depend on one's health, and certainly on one's survival, rationing health care equitably is particularly significant. Yet any mechanism of rationing must provide for the life and welfare of the sick and disabled whose medical care is likely to be more costly.

The first requirement for fair, decent, and equitable rationing is to provide health insurance for the 45 million Americans who do not have it. There is more. Equality of health care outcomes means inequality of health care dollars, for the healthy person requires less and the sick person requires more. A consensus regarding the amounts of money that should be allocated to health care is a political decision that should be made democratically. (Today it is largely made corpocratically.) The very wealthy and other haves may wish to spend money from their own pockets to underwrite their health. But surely this expense ought not be borne by have-nots (who are often also in poor health). Were the radical inequality of today to persist, it would be lamentable; that this inequality is supported by have-nots (directly and indirectly) is scandalous.

Yet greatly enhanced equality in outcomes is only part of the change required. Once long ago, or so the professional myth goes, physicians were gods. More recently, however, on June 23, 1999, the AMA voted that all its members be eligible for unionization, an open recognition that today physicians are largely bureaucratic functionaries and corporate employees. Not only do physicians feel the abrasiveness of corporate domination, but so do nurses, secretaries, receptionists, orderlies, and the numerous other employees of the health care system. At the bottom of this hierarchy of domination, perhaps under the illusion that they are the customers, are, of course, the patients.

As in other work situations, corporate domination of health care is unjust. The health care system must be democratic. (Even if physicians' unions prioritize their own salaries and working conditions, the situation of a unionized structure is, in principle, open to democracy, whereas current corporate structure is not. The increase in patients' medical and self-knowledge, the longstanding success of the book *Our Bodies, Ourselves*,[15] and other trends that betoken more democracy in health care are all signals that democratic organization in this undemocratic industry may be easier to achieve than we imagine.)

Although at times it is rational for us to grant physicians (and others) authority, it is never rational to grant authority without thought. Such authority, unfortunately, does exist and is more appropriately termed "domination" or "power." In the old days, too much authority went to physicians. Yet one often has no choice but to accept a physician's authority in terms of trusting his or her knowledge in prescribing essential drugs or performing surgery. The authority we give physicians, however, ought to be based on their skill, wisdom, and some shared agreement on values. Neither we nor physicians have reason to grant authority to HMOs, managed care insurance corporations, or any other bureaucratic, capitalistic organizations whose exercise of authority is not legitimate but rather is nondemocratic domination.

Unionizing physicians is a demonstration of democratic possibilities. Another significant reality is that women compose roughly half the current medical school enrollment. Further, the increasing use of the Internet to obtain medical information and to chat with others about treatment options has made medical information far more accessible. Education is as important for patients in the health care system as for citizens in civic society. In both areas, authority must be reasonable and must serve to benefit patients and citizens, respectively. Thus being a patient ought not to mean that one relinquishes one's rights as a citizen in a democracy. Overall democratic change must include democratic change in health care.

Many roads lead to democratic organization. To avoid these paths is to succumb to the corpocratic mythology of apathy, subservience, and natural inequality. Making health care more democratic may be easier than making other sectors of the corporate world democratic. (Who would ever have thought that the AMA would have countenanced unionization?) Good medicine and corporate domination are incompatible, and changing this situation may be easier than one might expect.

# 8    Children

Of course we were all once children. Most of us know children, and some of us work with them. Many of us act as though we know what is best for children (and for others); the media and some psychologists tell us to listen to the "child within us." What could be more straightforward than to understand children and to write about them? In the following pages, it becomes clear that certainty often gives way to likelihood, simplicity to complexity. Talk of children, as with members of certain other groups, often reveals more about those who do the talking than about the subjects themselves.

To begin, mythology must be shed. Children, as we know them, have not always been with us. Indeed, they are a rather recent phenomenon.[1] (A trip to a gallery of Western art will reveal that, surprisingly, until recently, children have been portrayed as nothing more than tiny adults.) Many children have never lived our conception of a child's life, most of them having been have-nots, having worked in agriculture and industry, having had little time for childhood as we know it.

Humans as a species are marked by unusual characteristics. Children are dependent on grown-ups, families, or communities for an extended period. Despite the pretensions of other primates, we are the only species capable of producing language. This is significant, for not only can children be taught to do as we do, but they can be taught to do as we and others say. In short, children can, and do, learn about the adult world, about their place in it, and about the necessary skills to survive. Some lessons, of course, are learned unconsciously, such as the child's need to bear and care for his or her own children.[2]

Children learn from their environments. These include families, schools, television, friends, even governments and corporations. Usually, perhaps inevitably, talk of changing (or improving) children's lives is directed not at children but at children's environments. Thus there are calls for better schools, quality day care, health care for children, more thoughtful families, even better family values.

Work is important to children in numerous ways.[3] The money a parent earns may be the family's only source of income. The father's income may be insufficient for the family, causing an increasing number of mothers to supplement their unpaid work at home with money from a paying job. Further, the number of single-parent families, with mothers at the helm, is increasing, as fathers, out of pressure or preference, keep their distance. In a single-parent family, the mother or, as described in chapter 4, the government may be the only source of income. Income in kind may also be furnished by grandparents, neighbors, or friends, or by bureaucratic organizations such as day care centers, schools, Head Start, or a plethora of not-for-profit agencies referred to by the elder president Bush's "thousand points of light."

Work affects children. Not only does it reduce the time parents have to interact with their children, but it may also alter the quality of their time together. For example, a parent who works for a corporation is likely to impart corporate values ("family values"?) to the child. The stress of work may be taken out on the child. Americans spend an average of sixty hours a week working, presumably needing or preferring what money can buy to spending time with their children. In short, work is likely to change the character of adults' interactions with most children, including even those of parents with their own children. (This, in fact, accounted in part for doing away with welfare, since not only work values, but also the values of welfare—depicted as slothfulness, promiscuity, not transmitting the connection of self-discipline to worldly reward, and so on—could be transmitted to children.)

The school environment is important to children. We are commonly cautioned that money should not be thrown away on social problems. (Public or private money directed at nonsocial problems is usually spoken of as money "invested," not thrown away.) The truth, however, is that inferior schools are likely to be underfunded and to exist in communities with poor tax bases and tight budgets. Such factors affect morale. Work with children is often underfunded, particularly in schools for have-not kids. Further, it seems an iron law of pedagogy that the younger the children, the lower the teachers' salaries and the fewer the investments in infrastructure. Thus teachers at universities usually earn more than those at day-care centers, in part because of supply and demand. Most university teachers are required to have Ph.D.s, and there are fewer Ph.D.s than certifications for day-care teachers. (It is noteworthy that many Ph.D.s specializing in child development agree on the importance of quality interaction with qualified adults at an early age, although the definition of quality is disputed.) I will return to this and other skewings of social investment presently, but even now it is apparent that something strange is at work regarding education, parenting, and health care; indeed, many investments in children demand explanation.

At one time, our infant mortality rate was extremely low, befitting a country with the most advanced medical care. However, we have now dropped through the median of infant mortality among developed nations. There is reason to be suspect of standardized bureaucratic tests, yet on standardized tests in mathematics and science American children do poorly compared with children of other developed nations. Is it any wonder that education was a significant issue in the 2000 election and in the following Congress? Certainly not, but only in small part because of scores on standardized tests. Baby boomers' children are now in school, and their parents worry about their children's education. Technology changes rapidly, and parents look to the schools to impart new technology to their children. Despite a plethora of labor-saving household gadgets, we have to work more hours to buy them, leaving us less time for our children. A medley of professionals has invaded the family and childhood—physicians, teachers, psychologists, social workers, even the dreaded dentist.[4]

Of course, "professionals" considered in the abstract mean little. Professionals issue from, are part of, and work in and for particular social environments. In the United States, these environments may exist in the gap between haves and have-nots, under the domination of corpocratic elites. After the frequent co-optation of professional training by corpocratic elites, what remains is a hypercommercialized society, even engulfing the professions, in which wisdom is replaced by expertise that, like other commodities, is for sale. Further, paid professionals in a patriarchal society infuse their expertise, broadcast their advice, and intervene. They work in a corpocratic public sector or in the not-for-profit sector or in the largely corporate private sector.

In concrete, professionals are pervasive, paternalistic, and increasingly put upon by bureaucracies that they may perceive as ensnaring them but that have-nots perceive as giving professionals clout. Some professionals are reactionary, dominating, and punitive. It is to the credit of many other professionals that they are ill at ease and interpret their jobs as helping their clients navigate the maze from which they have issued.

Professionals want to extend their influence and have been taught that they know more than parents do. Corporations make money from the American family in some measure through professions, as well as by selling children's clothing, through television and other media, investing in children as future consumers (recently visible in the sale of cigarettes), and cultivating children as future employees. Concern with patriarchal "family values" and violence in the schools—in short, with children—is most often refracted through families. (Typically violence had to invade middle-class suburbia in order to be recognized as a problem. In fact, middle-class violence often differs from violence associated with have-nots.)

By making childhood a problem, somewhere along the way we lose children's wisdom and playfulness; childhood no longer is seen as an end in itself but rather as preparation for future adulthood. Nowhere is this clearer than with the economic concept of "human capital."[6] According to this concept, childhood environments—from health care to school and even to organized play—should serve to increase the child's human capital. For example, teachers who actually find joy in educating or in playing with ideas are naive or deluded. As corporations know well, the goal of education is not to learn but to produce adults with increased human capital. Indeed, with the U.S. victory in the cold war, economic globalization, and the latest digital technology, increasing human capital in our labor force has become important for increasing the returns not only on corporate investments but in trade as well. In part, education has come to substitute for other social policy as the economy is exposed to global markets. Truly, human capital is currently among our scarcest resources. Augmenting human capital in the form of schools, training, and discipline is an additional encroachment on the welfare state as we know it.

The notion that children are resources for human capital trickles down from elite haves and permeates the rest of us, in significant measure because of professionals who enter the family. For example, educational test scores are rising among children of haves, other increases in human capital are quantified, and more substantial investments are made in those institutions where marginal returns to investment are perceived as greatest, such as the suburban schools of the children of haves. Never before have corporations so funded the formation of human capital required for current and future profits. Thus corporations cooperate with schools and the many professionals who guide our children, as is only sound investment practice. Indeed, corporations are taking over schools and education where they perceive profit. Typically in cooperation with the public sector, corporations find profitable ventures. For example, Channel One, complete with commercials, now further expanded into Extra Help, which allows children (whose parents may be working) to stay out of trouble after school while receiving help from teachers through interactive digital technology. Moreover, corporations may indirectly sponsor Little League, Pop Warner football, United Way, Boy Scouts, and Girl Scouts. Childhood, as we know it, is diminishing in our corpocracy.

We could continue to examine the external environments that affect children directly or through intermediaries like the family. Surely many dread the fact, or possibility, of drive-by shootings, gangsta' rap, violence on television, guns, and dangerous peer groups (recently described by Elijah Anderson in his book *Code of the Street*).[7] We could further talk about reconstruction that might improve these environments, as well as other issues. But we shall drastically limit our scope. It is worth noting, however, the influences corporations have even on unsuspected environments. For example, along with other media, television is owned by a shrinking number of growing corporations (which are becoming more global). The firearms industry has an obvious interest in more and better guns. One root of rap music was in the South Bronx, where it was often an expression of indignation, even protest. The co-optation of rap by giant media corporations like Sony and AOL Time Warner was swift and profitable (a cautionary tale for those who would change the external environments of childhood). Here I shall restrict the discussion to only a few of these external environments of childhood. Further, these are examples of environments where improvement is clear in principle, if difficult in fact.

One such environment is the family, an arena involving much psychological development. Yet we shall not consider psychology here except to note that while some fairly good ideas have been voiced about how a child might be destroyed, far fewer clues are offered on how to raise a child successfully. In this regard, we do know most definitely that there are many ways to raise a child and that the contemporary American family, even when headed by a single female, can be understood only in the context of patri-archy. Earlier it was noted that patriarchy was an important influence on professionals. Even more does patriarchy influence the family environment, and, as in the professional area, it does so both indirectly and directly. Such influences include male absence or the threat of it, family abuse by the male, male monopoly on decision making, and the male controlling and directing the family's finances. Indeed, some of these activities demand that professionals intervene immediately. Any consideration of the family as a concrete entity, instead of a dreamy abstraction, must recognize, and we hope change, such patriarchal environments. In chapter 10, on democratic change, nonpatriarchal society is more fully considered. In this chapter, however, attention turns largely to the family. Most families are patriarchal.

Many family struggles occur around money, more accurately its absence. Money, and the goods and resources it can buy, generally enhances family life. Money gives meaning to freedom of choice. (In our society, men, pa-ternal government programs, and male corporations have undue influence over money.) The best things in life may be free, but the many second bests require money. Haves have money. Have-nots do not. An overarching re-quirement in improving children's lives is to increase the cash, and in kind resources, available to families.

Most books on social policy do not consider the influence of taxes as social policy. The distinction between tax policy and policy for children and families, for example, is artificial. To begin with, taxes directly fund govern-ment social policy and indirectly subsidize not-for-profit social policy. Fur-ther, the current travesty where the rich get richer and the poor get poorer could be modified by redistributive tax policy. For starters, taxation should be more progressive. The Earned Income Tax Credit should be increased. Whether trickle-down economics is in some sense good is questionable. However, numerous provisions of our tax code, which are portrayed as good because they increase investment, do little of the kind. For example, IRAs promote minimal, if any, new investments. Rather, they shield existing in-vestments from taxes (one has to be a have even to contemplate an IRA).

The home mortgage tax deduction benefits primarily those who are wealthy enough to buy a house. One demographic result is the wholesale movement of haves to the suburbs, which geographically distances them from have-nots and the problems associated with them. (Another effect is that children going to inner-city schools, as opposed to suburban schools, have less tax money to improve their schools.) The vanishing estate tax deduction confirms that equality of opportunity is a rare exception to the intergenerational continuance of class, which is the American rule. Deductions for business expenses are consequential only for those in business. Corporate tax policy ensures that corporations do not bear their weight. The point seems evident: the current system robs from the poor and gives to the rich, perhaps a natural outcome of a tax policy highly influenced by haves, indeed, in part written by them.

Another overarching area amenable to private and public policy is work. Raising children is labor-intensive. Since only a minority of child care is cooperative, the general effect of child care is to free parents from raising their children and place the burden on underpaid, often unprepared young women. Thus haves pass child care on to have-nots in a further continuance of current class structure. (For example, under "workfare," states may train TANF mothers to be day-care workers, yet their own children are attending day-care centers.) Taxes could help here as well. Some have advocated substituting (or complementing) a consumption tax for (or with) an income tax, because a consumption tax would discourage consumption, which, in America, is increasingly for products once thought to be luxuries.[8] A consumption tax, compared with taxed market acquisitons, would also help make untaxed leisure time (including time spent with children) more attractive.

In today's America, a couple's decision to have children is, economically speaking, not an investment in the future, as it is in some countries and was here in times past. Instead, it is a losing proposition. The economic cost of raising children lowers the living standards of those families that choose to have children. (Indeed, the feminization of poverty is partially attributable to the costs of raising children.) Economically, having children today is no longer a solid investment, but a luxury. That adults frequently fail to appreciate this luxury is unfortunate. Instead, they turn to other luxuries, seemingly unaware that their families already coalesce around the luxury of children. This puzzle, of course, becomes more logical when one considers the message of the media: to sell products that are either wholly or in some measure luxuries.

But again (How often have we heard it?), children are said to be resources for the future. Although this may be true socially, it is not apt to be true for individual families. Yet this is the grounding for the government, corporations, and social services, which are taking over such "future resources" (newspeak for "investment") and leaving families, including single-parent families, yearning for the luxuries that corporations produce, promote, and sell. (This makes raising children even more expensive, since marketing is increasingly directed at them.) Indeed, as with tobacco, so it is with the media. As in Disney's "Small World" attraction, the children of the world are particularly favored commercial targets not only because the bulk of their consumption lies before them but because cartoons, puppets, even people in costume are both international and local at once, it being possible to translate their language, at little cost, according to location. In November 1999, the Disney Corporation announced plans for a $3.5 million theme park in Hong Kong, with Disney stars Mickey, Goofy, even Cinderella, speaking, of course, Chinese.

If this seems bizarre, it is only one of the many strange occurrences that arise in the meeting of corporation and family. To some extent, the economic disparity between corporations and families could be reduced by taxes—that is, by levying taxes on corporations for their use of the media and by granting significant tax credits (in effect, negative taxes) to families for their children. However, such a policy is not likely, as might be expected when the construction of social policies (including those involving taxes) are dominated by corporations. The general point is this: in addition to funding the government and the welfare state, taxes are a powerful tool to effect rational economic decision making. Unfortunately, the beneficent use of taxes for children and families only threatens to shrink further and goes virtually unmentioned in our corpocratic society.

Tax policy, being controlled by haves, who are thus more likely to take a deeper interest in it, grants, not surprisingly, a disproportionate number of tax breaks to haves. Corporations benefit from "corporate welfare," a particularly disagreeable piece of newspeak, as it largely diminishes other benefits to corporations in our political economy, which include government support of roads, medical research, and trade. In general, only haves command the resources required to manipulate the thousands of pages of tax codes; they have the power to insert language into these tax codes favorable to themselves.

Some of the disparity between haves and have-nots can be measured by money. This gap may be lessened by redistribution through the tax laws. Despite the frequent association of death and taxes, taxes are not inevitable or natural or God-given. Indeed, tax policy is authored by people in a fashion consistent with that discussed in chapter 1. Taxes are, of course, important because their manipulation affects the economy. Along with monetary policy and spending, taxes have been used to control macroeconomic policy. This use of taxes can help to ensure reasonably full employment, and it can also sacrifice full employment to prevent inflation, which is often of more interest to haves.

The alliance forged between corporations and the media has now become sufficiently solid that there seems no way out of it. On the surface, almost all we know of the world outside our immediate experience is provided by the generosity of corporations, whose advertisements pay for television, newspapers, and magazines, and which earn money from us whenever we pay for movies, sporting events, concerts, literature, and the like. Not only does the media inform us about the outside world, but it tells us how our own lives *ought* to be, even in what we cherish as our most intimate moments. In some measure, it is the media that teaches us how to express our feelings, what is funny and what is sad, how we should change our daily habits (such as the latest fashion we should follow), expectations about our sexuality, and so forth. The media is establishing dress codes and the ideals of physical beauty, femininity, and masculinity. For example, the wide teen emulation of MTV behavior, norms, and dress is almost sufficient to have co-opted adolescent rebellion and independence.

Unlike parents, the media changes quickly. Even middle-class youth work cheaply and long and hard hours to afford their versions of luxuries—expensive brand-name clothing, accessories, cigarettes, candy, and alcohol—promising that they, even more than their parents, will be exploited by corporations and enamored by luxuries. Examples abound of teenage girls who smoke and develop eating disorders to emulate the media's portrayal of the ideal body; of teenage boys "shaken down" or even killed for a particularly desirable jacket; of girls outfitted like Barbie dolls even though they have nothing to put in their purse; of boys with guns. These are not merely stereotypes, but profitable stereotypes.

The "serious" news was preoccupied with the minutiae of the race for the presidency well over a year before the 2000 elections took place, debated President Clinton's sex life, covered the O. J. trial from beginning to end, and was otherwise occupied with matters of equal consequence. Local news features neighborhood acts of violence, stories of distressed animals, and everyday folk talking about national stories such as these; it picks up national feeds, and the weather report slowly dribbles on. What is really important is usually not reported on the news at all. And when it is, most likely it is addressed in a manner consonant with corporate interests, this not out of conspiracy but because news people share information sources and public relations for the story covered, have been trained to be objective (disagreement therefore being within the parameters of professional objectivity), are often poorly paid and wish to be promoted, if possible before they need plastic surgery, hair dye, wigs, and the other appurtenances of youth.

How all this bears on childhood is profound. Children grow up in a world constructed largely by the media. Even for children, television is apt to occupy some three hours a day—and more important than the information the media provides is the understanding it presents of the world. The media even influences the way children play, advertising luxury toys and truly making children our most valuable future resources, training them not only in the ways of production but in the ways of consumption. All this, of course, assumes that children can be trained. As it happens, on this count American psychology may be correct. The more profound psychological insights— from Freud's theories of the unconscious to Chomsky's theory of an innate capacity for language to cognitive science's demonstrations that the black box of American behaviorism is not black and empty—show interesting structures worthy of study. Still, environments are important. Further, as stated earlier, environments are more amenable to outside influences and filter these influences to children. However, children themselves embody a hope that arises from some innate human nature.

Yet human nature, that of both adults and children, is submerged in corpocratic society. Let us attend here to one example, if at some length. In the media, the presence, and lack of, positive and negative role models have a pivotal place. We are told that negative role models include negative peers, the lack of authoritative fathers (perhaps particularly prevalent among poor African-Americans), and government benefits. We are also told that positive role models should be created by the family, especially middle-class white parents, strict teachers, and the "right" religion. As such, role models are contested and their existence has become pivotal to culture wars, racial and gender conflicts, and the politics of rich and poor.

A question is whether the media actually provides role models, especially negative role models as in rap music, videos, and violence, or whether these models mirror the actual experiences of many in the social world. Many media critics, talking heads, politicians, and other culture warriors assume that role models shape the substance of the young in particular. The notion of "role model" originally derived from the crevices of formal sociology. Here, the concept of "role" is rather common, and there is consensus about its meaning. Simply put, a role is a socially expected pattern of behavior, the part a person plays in social life. Of course, the word "role" was appropriated from the more venerable tradition of drama. Today, it is used in film, television, and other media of popular culture. For example, consider Danny Kaye's limitless imaginings in his starring role as Walter Mitty in the film adaptation of James Thurber's short story "The Secret Life of Walter Mitty." To have a *role* in life and in its projects is a universal desire. The media's evocation of role makes of it something more proximal and alluring than was the case even in drama, itself once a popular medium. Despite any ancestry in formal sociology, to most of us the meaning of our role is a product of the corporate media.

The notion of a "model" also is in formal sociology. Here, however, the term "model" has several meanings. One speaks of a model as a manipulable simplification that has a relationship, preferably operational, to the real world. Modern sociological models are predominantly quantitative. However, the use of the word "model" in the phrase "role model" points to a particular sort of model, the sociological role, which has a relationship, perhaps operational, to real people. In popular culture, such meaning dissolves into its precedents, like toy or miniature, which are manipulable versions of what they model. In modern mass media, the model is more apt to be manipulable by the media and by the corporation. Take, for example, the Model T and the many models of most modern vehicles. Computers, too, come in models, as do tract houses and televisions. Today, however, the most ready meaning of model is corporeal. In this incarnation, the model is usually a slender woman who models clothes and other instruments of seduction. The media has so pervasively used this model as the sexual bearer of stuff that too many women compare themselves with models, finding themselves deficient.

But on the trail of Barbie is Ken, both dolls. (Barbie was sold to parents as a role model for their daughters in an advertising campaign suggested by a psychiatrist consultant as a way to sell sexy dolls to young girls.) Male models are suave, athletic, and assured, and positive male role models include the Marlboro Man, Michael Jordan, Marcus Shankenberg, (the good) Bill Clinton, and Bugs Bunny. Role models communicated as negative include Tricky Dick(y) Nixon, Ted Kazynski, Charles Manson, Wile E. Coyote, and (the bad) Bill (Slick Willy) Clinton.

If the notion of role and model had a definite, if specialized, meaning in sociology, the meaning of their combination in popular culture is vague and ubiquitous. The expression "role model" has arrived full born into popular culture without any substantial incubation in psychology. Although the phrase is ubiquitous today, its imprecision will not stand scrutiny.

We would like to expect of words that they have some explicit relationship to reality. Unfortunately, here such coherent relationships do not exist. For example, any character or person who is a role model has an indefinitely large or infinite number of attributes or, at any rate, far too many to be copied or emulated. Therefore, presumably, only certain aspects of the role model are copied: the violence, the love, the clothes, and specific behaviors. Yet if this is the case, and it surely would have to be, how does one choose among the many attributes? In the talk and writing of role models, we find no guidance, quite naturally so because emulating role models is not an accurate or a meaningful description of behavior, action, and learning. Indeed, social learning is *active* learning, not the spongelike passive emulation of role models. There must be something in the nature of the "modeler," who somehow emulates the role model, to account both for the otherwise perplexing active selection of attributes from the potential model and for the active choice of model.

All this presupposes a relationship between people, specifically between modeler and model, a relationship that is unspecified and, in the loose language of role models, unspecifiable. In general, learning must be of something, must come from an active relationship with human or nonhuman environments, and it requires the learner's active participation. Active participation characterizes human development. The learner is not a passive sponge. Rather, human learning requires passion, emotion, and action. The mind as tabula rasa and other ideologies of the learner or modeler as passive sponge are inherent in the usual use of the notion of "role model," which is misleading, disingenuous, and false.

We are told that there are both positive and negative role models. The precise mathematical meaning of positive and negative dissolves into the imprecision of what is held to be socially desirable or undesirable (often socially desirable is code for the dominant sectors of society). Hence hip-hop beat hippies are negative role models, especially for corruptible and impressionable youth. Unfortunately, so the lore goes, some people, particularly those who are poor or otherwise marginal, lack not only money, access to health care, employment, even hope, but also access to positive role models. Indeed, often the many other deprivations are attributed to the lack of positive role models. However, if the notion of positive role model is as vacuous as suggested above, its lack can scarcely account for anything, including poverty and other marginalities.

The notion of "role model," meaningless though it may be, is set out authoritatively and confidently. And role models, to repeat, are usually thought of as either positive or negative, the media often being attacked for disseminating negative role models for which it repents with fixes like rating schemes, V chips, and net-nannies whose provision is to be taken as obviously self-evident of corporate responsibility. Rarely is the media asked serious questions beyond the scope of such technological fixes, although it is consistently asked of families, the youth, even public-school systems, objects of fashionable attack and manipulation.

The issue of violence perpetrated on our children is important for reasons extending well beyond the media's preoccupation with it into families' authentic concern with actual or possible violence against their children and into the corporate control of the two most commonly discussed reasons for violence, guns and culture (gross oversimplifications of complex phenomena). We ought not imagine that most violence against children takes place in schools or among their peers (e.g., the gang). Indeed, most violence against children is the action of adults. This includes not only child abuse, whose dimensions trivialize school violence, but automobile accidents, the violence of poverty, and the savagery of war (as inflicted on teenagers in our, or foreign, armed forces).

Certainly violence is an insult to a decent society. Any society striving to be respectable must be alert to the horrors of violence. According to Thomas Hobbes, people living in a violent state of nature where life was "nasty, brutish, and short" came together in a social contract in which they gave sufficient power to the state to control the most noxious violence. A decent society must be capable of controlling violence. To an extent our government does, but to a greater extent it does not. In fact, it even fosters violence. Violence includes children in its scope. For the most part, our's is a violent society. Violence is only enhanced by technological progress. Further, the bureaucratization of modern society serves to conceal all but the more flashy forms of violence, which the bureaucratic media defines as the *only* existing violence.

Of course, the most flagrant instance of violence is war. Here, with modest exception, such as the tragedies at My Lai and Andersonville, we maintain that we do not commit violence. Our soldiers know better. Often we show an uncanny resistance to their reports.[9] Further, we rarely think of the other side's casualties in war, counting only our own. Moreover, the "armies" of the global South contain an increasing number of boys with assault rifles. Once our families had many children and many sons. Today, most families have one son, maybe two. The loss of one son among many in war is painful. The loss of an only son is intolerable. The termination of the wars in Vietnam and Afghanistan were instances where such agony occurred to us and to the former Soviet Union.

Modern technology has made it possible to refine our military forces so that fewer Americans are killed in war, like in Desert Storm. The technology of the war in Kosovo allowed us a qualitatively new precision achieved by satellite-guided missiles and bombs (among other technologies) that allowed a war with casualties to Serbs and Kosovars while making our own casualties appear almost accidental. Here, our overwhelming display of mobile might ensured our continuing hegemony in Europe and the enmity of Russia and China, and projected our power to South America and Asia. (The Bush administration is more openly macho, "muscular," difficult, or belligerent.)

Why speak of war in a chapter on children? Until recently, this question need not have been asked, since our male children were obviously casualties of war. Today they are not (although children, women, and male noncombatants are, particularly in the long run because of the antiseptic devastation of the infrastructure). Yet even our children are harmed. The sheer money that advanced military technology requires is money lost for our children's needs. Children play with toy guns before acquiring real ones. They are bombarded with a media that uses violence to sell violent toys and to promote their acquisition. Both have and have-not children learn early the importance of having (recall the "luxury fever" of parents discussed earlier). Children learn the ways of a hyper-commercialized society, the unimportance of artistic and civic culture, and the significance of beating others in youthful competition. For example, high-school boys are urged on in football ("No pain, no gain"), and some girls become cheerleaders and others contestants in other sports, while medical studies show that especially the mild concussions sustained playing football result in increased learning disabilities, other more obvious injuries having already been acknowledged.

When violence exploded at Columbine High School in a privileged suburb of Denver, the media had an explosion of its own. Talking heads debated one another over the cause: Was it guns? Or was it a narrow definition of culture involving newspeak like "role model," overgeneralizations like violence, even the president having a meeting with minor Hollywood representatives? The reason for the turmoil was that violence had occurred not only among haves but in suburbia, the area specifically constructed so as to get away from have-not violence. Not only was this event an outburst of violence, but it was a betrayal of the American dream.

Consider that the two teen-age gunmen lived in a hermetic environment, played with children with whom they attended school and church, where they had jobs to help pay for their fancy cars. Like Small Town America, Littleton (literally, Little Town) was secluded and turned in on itself. Unlike Small Town America, it had been developed for precisely that purpose. The two boys in question had been out of the closet well before the incident took place. Other kids regarded them as a clique. They had a Web page. One was under psychiatric care. They were accomplished deadly shots, having trained on video games that used technology similar to military training technology. The two acted alone, having learned the requisite lessons from the Internet. The murder of their classmates was an adjunct to their own suicide. Both hated not only African-Americans but athletes, Jews, and numerous other groups—and they hated themselves, whom they also killed. The year after the incident, a newly aware, fortified, monitored, and retrained Columbine High School had racist graffiti scrawled on its walls. Since Columbine, there have been several other suburban white school shootings.

Can it be that professionals, talking heads, psychologists, and the police do not even know why the tragedy occurred or how to prevent others in the future? Is it possible that once in a while something goes wrong even in the most profitably planned of communities? Can what happened possibly be somehow connected with luxury fever, with suburban development, with kids working too hard, swayed by the same luxury fever as their overworked parents whose jobs were rendered less secure by corporate mobility?

Eventually, preferably later rather than sooner, children will grow up in our world, a world that has taken ever more care to teach children to be better consumers and producers than even their parents. Will the augmentation of corporate bureaucratic values only increase with each generation?

Children do not enter the world as vacant black boxes. Their minds and bodies are structured so as not to fit easily into such a dystopia. We ought to pay heed to this, indeed learn from our children. We should stop thinking of children as naive, childish, and rebellious, filled with hopeless idealism. Learning from children is indispensable for democratic change. (It is also a reason why parents close to children may have an edge over professional experts.) Of course, some children misbehave, at times frequently, sometimes savagely. And some parents, far too many, misbehave as well, even abuse their children. Child abuse, in its own right, is heinous; the legacy it leaves for the abused child as an adult is yet more heinous. In short, families are far from perfect. Although such imperfection in some measure rises from the constructed adult world, it must be dealt with. Indeed, it is an indictment of the current world that dysfunctional children and families, particularly among have-nots, are dealt with inadequately. Of course, there is a place for professionals, experts, even dentists. But that place must be held apart from routine professional intervention, ultimately at the behest of an adult corpocracy from which professionals act in the name of prevention.

Raising children to take part in a decent democratic society cannot occur simply within the family as a mini-democracy. However, authority should be used wisely and with informed observation not only of the child as a future adult but of the child as a child. Further, distribution within the family ought not to be by market principles, an excuse comparable to "spare the rod, spoil the child." Rather, children are best considered children who are members, indeed at the center, of the family.

How a society treats its children is arguably a desideratum of its morality. Our increase in infant mortality is appalling, and we should regard other societal factors (such as those discussed in this chapter) as unfortunate at best and requiring change. Indeed, democratic change is change toward a more authentically child-centered society, itself a valuable guide to other democratic change.

# 9　Outsiders

Alexander Hamilton was born and orphaned in the Caribbean, came to a land he would have part in fashioning as the United States, served on George Washington's staff during the Revolutionary War, married into a family of extreme wealth, impressed Washington sufficiently to be nominated as Secretary of the Treasury, and was killed in a duel by Aaron Burr. The story is familiar to us, not only with regard to Hamilton but as the American Dream (minus, of course, the early death).

Arguably, America has encouraged this dream, for ours was a rapidly growing country and the number of haves at its inception, even with slaves, was too small for the future. In the inner city, kids knew who Michael Jordan was and wore the Nike sneakers he promoted, shoes fabricated by have-nots in Third World counties. In truth, it is hard to live the American Dream and make it out of the inner-city ghetto, and the few who do, do so as individuals.[1]

In measure, America has fashioned its own way of dealing with have-nots. Particularly enlightened American haves have followed the path of enlightened European haves by allocating a small portion of resources to fund our welfare state. Today, the welfare state is shrinking, and its future is uncertain. Ironically, those most vocal in its shrinking invoke the language of opportunity and freedom — in short, the American Dream. This dream has been exported to Europe and the rest of the world, with developed countries also retrenching their welfare states, although Europe has more to retrench than the United States does. Nearsighted Europeans accuse us of never having had a welfare state. We accuse them of not having the American Dream, pointing to the number of their immigrants to America as proof, and we deem them "outsiders."

The previous chapters have dealt with different subsets of outsiders: poor, sick, and disabled people, each subset engaged from a different point of view. By so doing, it is hoped that readers have gained a measure of insight not only into the particular group discussed but also into the social, economic, and political world and ultimately the objective world the group inhabits. This chapter's title, "Outsiders," and the titles of many of the earlier chapters are examples of specific "categories." Debate as to whether categories are "objective," sound, even measurable or scientific or whether they are "subjective," constructed by society and power is ongoing. The claim of some postmodernists that all categories are socially constructed is extreme. So, too, is the claim of some philosophical realists that all categories are merely approximations to preexisting reality.

The dialectic over this issue entered the twentieth century with thinkers like Marx, Russell, Husserl, Levinas, and Foucault. Although we cannot engage that dialectic here, a few minor observations are in order. Some categories are objective, and others are constructed. More categories now appear to be constructed than was once the case. Deciding when a category is wholly constructed (simplistically "subjective"), partially constructed, or objective is a more complex undertaking than is appropriate here. (One neat consideration of these possibilities and their differentiation was made by the philosopher Wilfred Sellars in his essay "The Manifest and Scientific Image.")[2] Here we consider the categories of haves and have-nots as objective, not only in the Marxist sense, where they depict objective relations to the means of production, but also with some of the common sense that marked the philosophy of G. E. Moore. Thus to be hungry, to possess little—in short, to be a have-not—is objective and real even beyond Marx. To be able to command the resources of the modern world is objectively to be a have. Thus "have" and "have-not" are objective terms.

Objective terms often have socially constructed analogues, as in the categories named in the chapter titles. Indeed, the bureaucratic welfare state requires such constructed categories. In the end, the bureaucratic corporation that is displacing the welfare state deals with objectivity. In this chapter, I propose to reconsider the subjective categories that appear throughout these pages, to extend them, and to suggest the means of their construction. Not surprisingly, these subjective categories could have been constructed otherwise; indeed, they are always in motion. Here we speak of such wholly or partially constructed categories as elements of the more broadly constructed category of "insider" or part of the category "outsider." Reconsideration of the constructed categories presented in these pages is useful—not only subjectively but objectively as well. Thus in what follows we shall use the category of outsider for what it tells us about itself, about various groups that take on its categorization, and about those segments of society that construct the category. Further, we shall consider how the category of outsider has changed and will continue to change and how the boundaries between outsider and insider also change and how they are permeable, their boundaries even fungible.

In speaking of categories in this chapter, we speak of welfare, disability, social security, and health care; we also address being categorized as criminal, mad, homeless, substance abuser, and other such outsiders. Of course, such categories are socially, bureaucratically, economically, and politically constructed, theorized, altered, and so on. To receive public benefits from the welfare state, people must somehow be categorized as "outsiders." This chapter considers this case made with benefits surrounding disability. Although the chapter on health was not directed toward this point, sick people are temporary outsiders who are (or ought to be) eligible for welfare state benefits. Here we reconsider poor people, old people, and others categorized as outsiders. We also include those who are mentally ill, prisoners, homeless, and substance abusers with the expectation that the category outsider has something worthwhile to tell as well as to illustrate categorization in a changing welfare state.

The welfare state is under a precipitous assault that affects the categories it uses and those used by the global corporations that increasingly dominate and direct it, a domination achieving significant results. With regard to the elderly, welfare state benefits threaten to diminish and become privatized. With people who are ill, an overwhelmingly private sector has been corporatized, while the public segments of it, like Medicare, Medicaid, and the Veterans' Administration, are increasingly under corporate pressure. Poor mothers and children were recategorized as TANF replaced AFDC, the recategorization generally benefiting the corporate sector and harming many have-nots (including the working poor). Meanwhile, corporate, public, and not-for-profit policy have pushed haves farther away from have-nots.

Although the distinction between the the worthy poor and the nonworthy poor still legitimizes welfare state payments, payments are decreasing. Some point to the decrease as an achievement, the media often extols it, and the business press notes this extension of human resource management. Further, the receipt of public monies, even by the sick and elderly, has more stigma attached to it. Old people are portrayed as taking money from their children; sick people are processed by a bureaucracy more reminiscent of AFDC and SSDI than of medicine; and debates on euthanasia and physician-assisted suicide have increasingly active roles in discourse about disability and old age, penetrating even the deliberations to allocate resources by the World Health Organization in its quaint concept of "DALYs" (Disability Adjusted Life Years). "Quality of life" is an insidious piece of newspeak.

In significant measure, such distinctions among have-nots have disguised what have-nots share in common with one another and how their social situation differs from that of haves. The lack of awareness of social-class difference is an often noted oddity of discourse in the United States, most other nations having acknowledged class. Common, too, in the United States is an absence of class or an expansion of the number of classes in social scientific discourse, thus reducing the distinction between haves and have-nots. Political and social discourse often speaks of waves of immigrants, with interests that transcend their class.[3]

The Horatio Alger myth, according to which one goes from rags to riches, is unusual when compressed into one generation. Extend the myth to two or three generations and add what Americans are perhaps most proud of, the chance of upward social mobility, and the myth can become fact. And there are other elements: the frontier[4] being an ocean away from Europe and Asia, natural wealth, never having fought bloody class revolutions, no feudal past.[5] This said, we are a natural experiment, the first new nation,[6] a people of plenty,[7] a land where cowboys outsmart Indians as surely as the good guys beat the bad guys.[8]

To social science and to a media tied to corporations, discussion of an America composed of two classes was seen as hopelessly naive. If such discussion was engaged in by Alexander Hamilton, James Madison, and other Founding Fathers,[9] it preceded discussions informed by the social sciences. However, even before our founding, the distinction between the worthy poor and the unworthy poor arrived in America with English immigrants. But this distinction, which came to underlie our welfare state[10] and to assume a convenient and pervasive autonomy in voiced and unvoiced American discourse, was a distraction from the dichotomy of class in both thought and fact: it set one segment of poor against another, and it created a complex tapestry that covered the distinctions between haves and have-nots.

Today corporate capitalist power threatens the welfare state as we know it (just as the state, under its dominance, recently threatened welfare as we knew it). The acquisition of corporate power over and through the state is congruent with the interests of haves. Contemporary culture and media are directed toward corporate interests, a fact haves rarely resist. As illustration, let us consider some groups that are usually not grouped together. To the disabled, the sick, the poor, and the elderly, let us add prisoners, the mentally ill, and the homeless. Changes in bureaucratic categorization create a certain interchangeability among these categories of outsiders. Indeed, the categories are fungible. Almost all such people not only are members of the constructed category of outsider but are members of the objective category of have-not. Consider the following example:

> The 16-year-old girl suffered from delusions and hallucinations. The diagnosis was "psychotic, not otherwise specified." Her father was in prison for sexually abusing her sister. Her mother was an alcoholic. Not surprisingly, the girl began skipping school. She got pregnant. She assaulted her mother. Before most state hospitals were closed, the girl would probably have been committed to a state psychiatric hospital. But in Texas, where she lives, the juvenile court declared her a delinquent and sent her to the state's juvenile justice agency, the Texas Youth Commission. The commission sent her to its Corsicana Residential Treatment Center for the seriously emotionally disturbed youths. The girl personifies the problems facing many young people with mental disorders, said Linda Reyes, a psychologist and assistant deputy executive director of the TYC [Texas Youth Commission], "Unless you are wealthy and can afford private doctors, you have to get arrested to get treatment," she said.[11]

Welfare state categories of the criminal and the mentally ill are fluid, constructed, changeable, and porous. Of the almost 2 million prisoners in the United States, estimates are that 200,000 to 1 million have a major mental illness. A survey released by the Department of Justice on July 11, 1999, confirmed the prison's role as mental hospital: "An estimated 283,800 mentally ill offenders were held in the nation's state and federal prisons and local jails at midyear 1998, according to a special report released today by the Justice Department's Bureau of Justice Statistics (BJS). An additional 547,800 mentally ill people were on probation in the community."[12] Some experts place the percentage far higher, particularly since the Department of Justice counted only those prisoners who identified themselves as mentally ill. More than three-quarters of the prisoners had been in jail before, mentally ill prisoners spending an average of fifteen months longer in jail than their sane counterparts—perhaps because mental illness can get one into trouble in prison. In 1955, mental institutions, often wretched, held 559,000 people, a number that dropped to 69,000 in 1995.[13] Further, the proportion of prisoners with personality disorders, mood disorders, and other afflictions cited in the fourth edition of the *Diagnostic and Statistical Manual of Mental Disorders* (*DSM-IV-TR*) is surely no less than among those not in prison.[14]

Once asylums looked like prisons. Then and now, prisons are not conducive to mental health, although they are effective in separating prisoners and mental patients from the rest of us. Deciding whether an outsider is a criminal to be imprisoned or a person who is mentally ill and needs to be hospitalized continues to be perplexing and changeable. Although the Mc-Naughton Rule greatly narrowed the category of criminally insane, requiring only that a perpetrator know the nature and consequences of the act, many more prisoners are mentally ill by a more generous *DSM-IV-TR* categorization of mental illness. A greater proportion of African-Americans are sane prisoners. Dorothy Otnow-Lewis, a psychiatrist, attributed this to white psychiatrists "being very bad at recognizing mental illness in minority individuals."[15]

Mentally ill patients in state prisons were more than twice as likely to have been homeless than other inmates before their arrest.[16] Like substance abuse, homelessness changes fluidly, even arbitrarily, as a category making one liable to arrest. Like substance abuse, homelessness has many causes, from mental illness to a lack of affordable housing. The police even arrest homeless people out of kindness, realizing that they may well have no other place to go (say, on a dangerously cold night). Homelessness has changed from its original evocation of sympathy, however, into evoking frequent public hostility. "Jails have become the poor person's mental hospitals," said psychiatrist Linda A. Teplin.[17]

On an average day, it [the Los Angeles city jails] holds 1,500 to 1,700 inmates who are severely mentally ill, most of them detained on minor charges, especially for being public nuisances . . . jail, by default, is the nation's largest mental institution. . . . what experts call the criminalization of the mentally ill has grown as an issue as the nation's inmate population has exploded and as corrections officials and families of the emotionally disturbed have become alarmed by the problems posed by having the mentally ill behind bars.[18]

Mental illness is spoken of in many ways. In religious terms, it may be a consequence of possession by spirits. Morally, it may represent evil, perhaps evidence of original sin. Biologically, it may be the result of disease or genetics. Psychologically, it may be learned or be a deficiency in learning. Psychoanalytically, it may be a disorder of the mind. Sociologically, it may emerge from socialization, environmental influence, or marginalization. Economically, it may be owing to poverty, restricted employment opportunity, and so on. It may arise from nature, nurture, or both. However, corporations, bureaucracies, and the public care little about such niceties of mental illness, except insofar as they have direct experience with it. Mental illness is still substantially in the closet. Further, much mental illness is a nonproblem, because either it is being treated with drugs or drugs are effectively zoning out problematic behaviors. Yet prisons are a growth industry, mental illness is still held by many as immoral, and the criminal justice system can serve more purposes than can the more narrow mental health system. For outsiders, including homeless people and substance abusers, prisons have eclipsed mental institutions, rehabilitative services, and other specialized institutions.

What some older societies did to punish crime differs from punishment for crime in modern Anglo-Saxon society, the former having a range of punishments seemingly designed to fit the crime, the latter ostensibly having recourse to only various lengths and degrees of incarceration, except for extreme crimes that may be punishable by death.[19] Punishment, however, is not the only way to deal with crime, an alternative being prevention. Thus banks are more secure than restaurants, social workers make police less ubiquitous, and so on. Further, prevention may be directed at potential criminals. (For example, death was a means of preventing crime in the eugenics common to the first third of the twentieth century. In the United States, death was interpreted by some to include abortion, infanticide, even birth control. In Nazi Germany, a more generous variant of eugenics included execution, eventually mass execution. One wonders: Will the unraveling of the genetic code lead to a newly refined eugenics?)

More commonly, crime prevention is coupled with another external cause, such as the environment, the family, school, or drugs. Thus crimes committed by the poor are prevented by programs and policies of income maintenance, education, and social welfare. Sometimes crime may be prevented by removing the potential criminal from an environment that engenders crime through such devices as foster care or adoption. Some say that punishing criminals is a deterrent to others contemplating a criminal act. Petty crime is often said to lead to more serious crime. One version of prevention even penetrates the family, with parents being told that "sparing the rod spoils the child." Others view punishment as leading to redemption. Thus torture leading to confession could be redemptive.[20] Today, some believe that incarceration is a time for rehabilitation.

The outsider category is obligatory to the bureaucratic corporate welfare state, the outsider considered a welfare state version of a category of greater and more direct interest to corporations: the nonemployable. Bureaucratized categorization is necessary in domains like immigration, welfare, childhood, old age, and disability. Distinctions like worthy poor and nonworthy poor are also necessary for the welfare state. Welfare state distinctions enhance and rank categories of outsiders. Professionals are there to work with outsiders or to function as intermediaries between insiders and outsiders, including lawyers, physicians, social workers, teachers, and police.

Consider substance abusers and the elaborately fluid choice of who qualifies and how they are to be treated. Almost any substance can be abused—air, for example, by hyperventilation. Polydypsia, or water intoxication, is a problem among some psychiatric patients. The first task in the establishment of substance abuse is what substances count. Air doesn't count. What does count has changed across cultures and historically. A significant part of this history is the proliferation of substances. Amphetamines, many sedatives, even heroin are reasonably new. Heroin, despite its efficacy against pain, is not available even by prescription in the United States. The opiate of last medical resort for pain is methadone, a drug also prescribed for the rehabilitation of heroin addicts. Alcohol became illegal but was then legalized again. Over the years, alcohol abuse has gained substantial professional attention and, indeed, was defined as a disease during this last period of its legalization.

Most Americans are caffeine addicts, craving at least one cup of coffee a day. Giving up caffeine is difficult, brings on headaches, and may leave former addicts feeling sleepy. (Brits prefer their boost in the form of tea, a preference now shared by many.) Since American folklore has it that coffee stunts children's growth, kids get their fix from Coke or Pepsi or even caffeinated Mountain Dew and Dr Pepper, which elude the scrutiny of invasive parents. (This notwithstanding, the mean height of American children has increased, as has their weight, the latter partially a result of substantial amounts of sugar, arguably an abused substance, in soft drinks.)

Nicotine is a physiologically addictive substance. Cigarette use currently shortens the life span of Russian males by eight years. The most desirable cigarettes in Russia and the world are exported by American multinational corporations, currently under some pressure in their native land. Nicotine was not revealed as a drug, however, until tobacco corporations, under injunction, released reports clarifying that they were indeed engaged in a conspiracy to hook new nicotine addicts. Illegally abused substances such as cocaine, crack cocaine, marijuana, heroin, and hallucinogens, originally confined to ghetto African-Americans and hippies, penetrated the communities of haves.

There is a significant overlap between prisoners and the mentally ill, which results in these individuals reverting back and forth between the two categories. The overlap between mental illness and substance abuse has its own category: the Mentally Ill Chemically Addicted (MICA). The overlap between prisoners and those with a history of substance abuse is substantial. Significant overlaps are a consequence of available substances used by the mentally ill to self-medicate; for example, individuals who are suffering from anxiety or depression may self-medicate with alcohol. Not only substance abusers but homeless people inundate the prison system. Young African-American males are overrepresented, while rich haves are only rarely in jail.

Successful prevention and treatment programs extending into the Nixon administration were displaced by interdiction and punishment as we embarked on the war on drugs, a war that became downright silly during the Reagan administration when the First Lady advised that we "just say no." The war on drugs has imprisoned a far higher proportion of users who are people of color than who are white. Indeed, a disproportionate amount of prison space is occupied by African-Americans convicted of nonviolent drug-related offenses, a costly use of our prisons. Thus there is substantial overlap between two categories of outsiders—substance abusers and prisoners—with less but significant overlap with African-Americans.

The war on drugs has been a failure. Some combination of legalization or decriminalization of substances, in combination with attention to environmental factors, mental illness, prevention, and treatment, would be a more rational approach. Further, it is mere common sense to improve the economy of the ghetto and the general education of high schoolers—in short, to address many problems of have-nots.

Although the war on drugs failed to achieve its stated purpose, it succeeded in legitimizing an increasing number of police, giving police increased access to technology, even curtailing civil liberties. It also facilitated coordination between law-enforcement offices once separate—like the local police, the Federal Bureau of Investigation, the Drug Enforcement Agency, Alcohol, Tobacco, and Firearms, the Central Intelligence Agency, the National Guard, the armed forces, the Coast Guard—all now increasingly interconnected with one another through high-bandwidth digital telecommunications and to increasing information increasingly integrated. The war on drugs is an important part of our foreign policy. As a recent example, in the year 2000, $1.3 billion was set aside for the Colombian war on drugs, including $1.1 billion for military matters. This vast sum was at least partially aimed at fighting people, not plants. These and future developments threaten life, privacy, and liberty. But a corpocracy is more concerned with protecting the rights of corporations than with protecting the rights of outsiders.

Some students of social policy state that in the past it was the disruption of have-nots, or the threat of their disruption, that forced progressive policy change, particularly by disturbing the middle class so it would demand change from the government out of fear, compassion, and a preference for order.[21] Accordingly public policy is changed by haves worried about the threat of have-nots. (Such change is not without danger, of course, having accounted not only arguably for the New Deal in America but for Nazism in Germany.) However, today the state has developed ingenious technologies of social control. For example, the urban riots during the Johnson administration led to the Kerner Commission, which suggested numerous ways to better the lives of have-nots. But the urban disruption following the violent arrest of Rodney King inspired new strategies, new technologies, and further coordination among the armed forces, the National Guard, the FBI, and local police departments. As the verdict for the police officers indicted in the Rodney King beating was handed down, police presence was evident, particularly in dangerous neighborhoods. The National Guard stood ready in a stadium nearby. Preparations had been made to prevent and to contain any violence by have-nots.

Techniques of nonlethal warfare have been developed for use both abroad and at home, as tear gas has been supplemented by rubber bullets, super-amplified music, psychological warfare, as well as "exploding nets, nausea-inducing ultrasound weapons, blinding laser lights, incapacitating (and potentially asphyxiating) sticky foams, and quick drying substances that can be used to seal doors."[22] A private shopping mall in Australia successfully used the music of Bing Crosby and pink acne-revealing fluorescent lighting to disperse groups of undesirable teenagers. In the future, police may replace social workers, the FBI may replace lawyers, and the armed forces may replace other more benign social policy.

The war on drugs has led to the advance of technologies of domination at home and has contributed to suppression of democracy abroad. Thus we have trained and supplied the troops of Latin American governments to assist us in the war on drugs at their point of origin. It is difficult to eliminate powerful cartels well represented in governments and change the behavior of poor peasants whose only way of life is to grow coca, opium poppies, and marijuana. However, these U.S.-equipped troops have overturned popular elections and eliminated popular resistance to authoritarian regimes. Thus the war on drugs has assisted the power of client regimes obligated to the United States with armed forces led by U.S.-trained officers using weapons made by our corporations. The examples of Colombia, Peru, and Mexico in this hemisphere suffice.

Drugs frequently arrive from countries with regimes significantly supported, if not made possible, by U.S. intervention. Internally, the war on drugs has legitimated the policing of our country, has contributed to the abrogation of civil liberties, and has led to overcrowded jails because of the imprisonment of nonviolent drug offenders, more easily imprisoned than rehabilitated. What Michel Foucault termed the "carcerial state" is often more "cost-effective" for corporations than is the welfare state.

Substance abuse and the war on drugs are instructive examples of the welfare state being replaced by a carcerial state, a subject of substantial current importance, its significance only promising to increase in the future. Many future possibilities, such as home imprisonment (in which "inmates" wear leg bracelets to broadcast their location), large computer databases, and other technologies currently unforeseeable, may make the carcerial state seem a preferred way of dealing with matters currently handled by the welfare state.

Narrow thought leads to cheaper, more affordable, and tougher programs, programs for the greater good of haves. One example was the modification of the AFDC into TANF, the end of welfare as we knew it. The devastation of Social Security approaches a looming horizon. The artifact of the new millennium is an additive in exploding a change in welfare state programs. Nonemployable has long been a category of consequence to corporations (and, to a lesser extent, to public education outsourced by them to the government), relieving corporations of the burden of case-by-case decision making.

As machines increasingly took over production, the United States fashioned a system of compulsory public education. Today, as computers take over many of the functions once performed by people, the nature of employment again changes. On-the-job education and reeducation have augmented one-shot education according to corporate requisite. Technologies change. Further, corporations can more easily draw employees to areas of low crime than high crime, of good education than inferior education, such "quality of life" issues being addressed by a seemingly corporate charity (newspeak for "self-interest").

Changes in our welfare state are to be expected, including greater unemployment benefits to give prospective employees sufficient time and means to search for jobs where they are of most use to corporations, expanding day care as women become increasingly important employees, even providing a form of universal health care, a further enabler by corporations of the government to take over programs external to corporations as demands for job flexibility increase. Such future welfare state extensions may be private or privatized.

Production, including the part of it attributable to human beings, is of concern to corporations insofar as goods are sold—that is, insofar as production and consumption lead to a maximization of present and future profit. Profit does not come from production alone, and production does not automatically bring about consumption. Of course, consumption had been encouraged earlier, a particularly exemplary corporate encouragement being made by Henry Ford, who offered enough pay and credit to his workers to be consumers of the Model T in a dazzling contribution to our country's social and economic evolution. However, this contribution did not take into account that more Fords could be produced than could be bought. It was not until the Keynesian evolution that a solution was found; government takes up the slack when there is too little private demand. Keynesian economics was not consistently applied in the United States until the arms industry demanded more products from private industry and employed an increasing number of workers as soldiers in World War II. When we won the war, demand from the military sector supplemented pent-up consumer demand. The public military sector was funded by what President Eisenhower termed the "military–industrial complex." Government was the consumer of military production. Finally, we won the cold war.

Still, such ongoing threats as drugs, rogue states, and minor uprisings threatening to become major, the expansion of treaty obligations (e.g., NATO's from a defensive posture to an offensive posture), and the success of new military technologies all ensure that our government will continue to be a consumer of military material, research, and development, as will foreign buyers of our military technology. Meanwhile, our military technology will continue to be the best in the world under considerably government-funded research and development, as well as contracts for still undeveloped military goods and services like Star Wars, the popular name for the Strategic Defense Initiative, now revived to protect us from rogue states (Once, we are told, the threat of its development and deployment helped lead toward our victory in the cold war.) Thus the ultimate outsiders of the Evil Empire were replaced piecemeal by the elevation of other outsiders.

More can be said about the development of the category of customer to complement that of producer in corporations, the expansion and coagulation of the category of buyers into a market where corporations compete for an increasing market share of a growing pie by productivity gains, money saved by reductions in welfare programs, money extracted from employees by low wages, automation, and foreign labor. Consumption has increased, and our private savings rate is negative — we spend more than we earn. The interest on these debts goes to haves, and the discipline it imposes on workers helps make labor more "flexible."

Further refinement of a consumer market is straightforward. On average, we watch almost four hours of television a day. Both haves and have-nots see the consumption habits of haves, frequently of celebrity haves, and of powerful haves who inspire haves and have-nots to new consumption. Elaborate research is devoted to television viewing. Television is governed by the disposable income controlled by viewers, a function of the number of viewers and their demographic categories. Commercials are produced with more care than the programs that sell them. (The transfer of public air waves to the private sector, a transfer matched by the sale of the government evolved Internet to the private sector amplified by the Telecommunications Act of 1996, is a further example of government accepting many of the risks of research and development, turning over those that succeed, like the Internet, the microchip, and the jet, to the private sector as gifts called "spinoffs," sometimes used to justify public investments.)

Markets are created not only by television but by the Internet, the press, and other media protected by the First Amendment, which tell us both sides in a free market of ideas dominated by transnational corporations. We buy more or less the same products as our neighbors do. Our need for automobiles is guaranteed by the suburbs. Credit helps, and easy credit helps more. Whether people are perceived as consumers is significant to the media. For example, the *New York Times* is rarely for sale in the South Bronx; further, in the fall 1999 network television lineup, the number of African-Americans in lead dramatic roles dwindled. The category of consumer is essential to the bottom line of corporations, has contributed to the public relations and advertising industries, and has advanced social science research.

A federal corporate bureaucratic welfare state devolves to the nether worlds of state, county, and local government, and is often privatized by corporations along the way. Indeed, as of 1999, state governments spent fewer federal welfare dollars on welfare than they received, the number of recipients having undergone a miraculous decline owing to Draconian schemes of recategorization and reallocation. Much of the surplus went to nonprofit-related programs, some even to "pork." In the 2000 elections, politicians outbid one another in taking credit for having reduced the number of welfare recipients.

Welfare state categories, which linger to construct elements of already decreased relevance, threaten to be subsumed into objective subcategories. Some version of the constructed category of outsiders will remain so as to ensure a righteous cloak for the more rigorous and important categories like that of consumer, already under corporate domination (although corporations argue among themselves as to whose products people should consume). The most vital category, that of producer, will become unabashedly important as corporations dominate the state, privatize public functions, and transform them, and as the increasing power of corporations makes it even more obvious that the corpocratic sector is the one from which important policy emerges.

Growing transnational corporations increase corporate power over the public and not-for-profit sectors; increase spending, particularly by powerful corporations in powerful countries; and enhance the skilled use of propaganda, public relations, and the media. The corporate domination of the state, which indeed defines a corpocracy, makes the notion of changes in public policy as a result of have-nots threatening haves less plausible. Should this happen, it will be a complement to corporate domination of the state, a state in which citizens have no say either in corporate policy, as is true today, or in public policy, including social policy. Such scenarios are not inevitable and call for increasing organization among citizens to regain control of their government—in other words, to reestablish democracy.

In 1999, the United Nations Development Programme published a report on new development marking sixty countries as worse off than they were in 1980. "Global inequalities in income and living standards have reached grotesque proportions," noted the report, which also claimed that Ford's annual sales generated more income than Saudi Arabia. The report viewed future technology as making inequality only more gruesome. For example, an American can buy a computer with one month's salary, whereas a Bangladeshi must work for one year to afford one. Moreover, there are cultural offshoots from telecommunications technology. For example, 80 percent of Web sites are in English.[23]

In the future of our welfare state, the category of outsider will not be constant. Indeed, it promises to change more rapidly than it already has historically. Rather, it will vary according to changes in social policy. If such change continues essentially to be for the worse, outsider category changes will favor sticks over carrots, prisons over prevention, and policing that increasingly enforces prevailing distinctions between insiders and outsiders. Further, the category of outsider will be subject to changes that reflect those of transnational corporations, automation, globalization, hard and soft technologies, and the practices of our welfare state and how it mirrors and complements bureaucratic corporate capitalism. Meanwhile, without a politics that challenges the objective conditions from which they issue, the objective categories of have and have-not will remain and only grow more disparate.

Such gaps may worsen without conscious political organization by people. But this chapter is not written in stone. If history influences people, then just as surely people influence history. Yet, unlike past history, our future history is unwritten and can still be changed.

# 10 Democratic Change

By now, readers are perhaps asking what is to be done. While it is impossible to provide a road map of the future, consider these closing pages as one possible route toward democratic change.

Historically, democratic change is not inevitable, nor does it come by flipping a lever (even in a voting booth). Further, it cannot come from the top down, as is currently true of much social policy. Indeed, democratic change is not just a goal but an instrument.[1] The process and achievement of necessary change must be democratic.[2] Too often, purportedly necessary change has come from the domination of a philosopher king,[3] a party,[4] an expert class, a bureaucracy,[5] or a military force.[6] Such yellow brick roads have led to permutations of the organizational forms that guide them. We are told that violence was necessary for peace, torture for redemption, destruction for construction, and discipline for freedom. But the structures used to establish a regime endure. If we are to expect a democratic future, it must be achieved democratically.

Democracy is not restricted to the vote. Further, the United States is more a corpocracy than a democracy. Almost every country in the world calls itself a democracy. If South America is democratic, if the now defunct Eastern bloc was democratic, surely we more than qualify. But these are hardly examples of what is meant here by democratic: direct rule of civic society exercised of, by, and for the people. Such democracy is rare and difficult to achieve, but it is hardly impossible. The liberty we expect is hard to come by and requires constant vigilance, but liberty is also far from impossible.

The project of bringing about democratic change must include a critical analysis of what has already existed, or else the future may well be the outcome of nondemocratic arrangements, thought, and domination. It is my hope that this book has exposed a range of social policy to critical thought. It is important that such critical thought also recognizes the good, such as Social Security, Medicare, the Earned Income Tax Credit, and so on, as well as the bad. Critical thought is often made difficult by contemporary education, the media, propaganda, public relations, and self-interest. Penetrating through these obstacles is essential for democratic change, if not for a sane life. Some ways to accomplish this are through study groups, education, experience, and collective action. Further, the helping professions must be rethought and reformed. The press reveals much of what pundits seldom comment on, which, although sometimes tricky to find, is usually there.[7] Further, it is important to decode the words of pundits for the propaganda they often are, to recognize the workings of propaganda,[8] and to understand its connections to advertising, profit, and corporations.

As suggested earlier, the modern media, propaganda, and public relations massively control our information and understanding. They can even affect the way we think, particularly when their myths correspond to the bureaucratic corporate structures that govern much of our lives. Two myths are particularly pernicious and prevalent. The first is the myth of the market, which holds that the market is natural and the best approach; its expansion is to be welcomed and, at worst, inevitable; it is progressive and allied with democracy; and market freedom is equivalent, or superior, to other freedoms. The second myth concerns our political lives and tells us that our political lives are more confined than is the case; voting between Tweedle Dee and Tweedle Dum is our highest civic duty; such votes demonstrate our freedom of choice; significant political action is not political action but deviant behavior; changing the system from without is at best futile, at worst destructive, and precludes political action involving authentic forms of education, organization, and affiliation; in short, that our political lives truncate the political into a parody of itself. Of course, a corollary to this is that any attempt to bring about real change is futile, and we are reduced to being cynics, pessimists, quasi-hermits, and consumers: from political beings into apolitical spectators and market activists.

Many issues, however, invite political organization. They may be encountered at work, in our children's schools, or by following thought into democratic political action. At least two domains where such issues have emerged in these pages are vital, and they are bureaucracy and corporations. The artificiality, domination, transfer of resources from have-nots to haves, and frequent connections among these elements are important. Bureaucracy is a means of domination, a way to grind people up, and affects our lives outside the bureaucracy. Corporations are complex organizations of dominance,[9] in which haves control have-nots. Immortal sovereign corporations break the bonds of nationality into transnational paradise. Corporations are authoritarian, if not totalitarian.[10]

Corporations and bureaucracies are unreasonable entities to be resisted. However, we are not sanguine about merely quelling their power. Currently, political systems are outpaced by rapidly developing markets. We expect that, more likely, the power of the political state can reemerge as more powerful than that of even global markets and corporations. Too many counter-examples exist to regard corporate and bureaucratic dominance as a given. Realistically both can, and should, be challenged democratically as nondem-ocratic organization and government. Some moderate proposals for decent progressive change have been suggested earlier in our discussions of Social Security, health, taxation, and poverty. Although modest, such changes may be surprisingly difficult as we are losing control of our government. Thus part of our efforts must be to reclaim the state, since the government is the only organization potentially sufficiently powerful to control corporations.

Most policy, including social policy, is made by haves. The welfare state has been pummeled, and social policy is under assault. Haves are over-whelmingly corporate, economic, and political elites. It has been useful to coin a word to describe this sort of government, as the terms "democracy," "meritocracy," even "plutocracy" miss the mark. Rather, the neologism "cor-pocracy" best describes the sort of government that now prevails in the United States. The ugliness of the neologism is apparent, and thus only appropriate.

Modern successes against corporations and bureaucracies have occurred at such diverse points as the United Parcel Service strike, an effective popular resistance to the corporate Multilateral Agreement on Investing, the decen-tralization of the public school system in South Chicago, the achievement of civil rights legislation like Title IX for women and Title VI for African-Americans, the Americans with Disabilities Act, localized resistance to WalMart and gargantuan new shopping malls, not voting (when it helps delegitimize a corpocratic government), the events in Seattle, and more. However, to reconstruct life as a citizen is not without risk, nor is it without effort. Aristotle's definition of human beings[11] as being essentially political must be reclaimed. Traditional notions of freedom must be revived, of justice reasserted, and of community reaffirmed. Current violations against the environment, indigenous peoples, and the rights of have-nots ought to be stopped and reversed. Land, labor, and capital ought not be regarded as commodities, but rather as fundamental qualities essential to human existence.

Offered here is one version of democratic change issuing from our critique of the assault on social policy. Perhaps economic change has been overemphasized, but economics is indeed part of politics, as was made clear in the critique of bureaucracies and corporations. Indeed, social justice requires economic justice, and political democracy requires economic democracy. It is worth repeating that, politically, our country is less of a democracy, a plutocracy, or a meritocracy than it is a corpocracy.

What we expect of a polity includes what we expect of our political economy: a high measure of efficiency. We do not wish people to work hard for nothing, or almost nothing. Nor do we wish resources to be squandered. We expect there to be a safety net so that being out of work does not mean starvation, homelessness, or other outrageous fortunes. Further, since people should not have to beg for their survival, we expect such a safety net to be a matter of right, not public largesse or private charity. We do not expect workers to be wage slaves but to be able to express a substantial measure of freedom in and through their work. Thus we expect that work not be incarcerating, whether by a boss, the bureaucracy, an assembly line, the fear of being fired, and the like. Indeed, since people come together in work, we expect work to enhance civic virtues, not to be a hiatus from such virtues. We agree with Freud about the importance of love and work and expect that the two be connected. To a great extent, we expect people to like their work. We expect that economies be integrated globally for the benefit of people, not of corporations. Inevitably, this will require more effective and more democratic international political arrangements as well as democratic organization around the globe.

The market is a tool, subservient to conscious democratic politics. Decisions of what are and what are not to be market commodities; when, where, and how to regulate them; policies of taxation; and the various social policies discussed in this book must be open to continual democratic change. Equality of opportunity is routinely expected and promised. Still, one expects there to be substantial equality of results. The present difference between haves and have-nots is unacceptable, and that this difference may well increase in the future is monstrous. Democracy is to be expected in the organization of work, and hence so too a diminution of bureaucracy, hierarchy, and domination. Leisure, too, should be democratic, if only because the lessons of work are complexly transferred to the conditions of leisure, and so the two are related.

Such expectations are not at odds with others equally reasonable, are not internally contradictory, and are justifiable. One expects all these and more from the polity, economy, and other organizations. Moreover, organizations should be nourishing of freedom, responsive to people, and respectful of the rights of minorities. These and other expectations should not violate further expectations of the polity and society. It is essential to discern ways to get from here to there, ways that surely may not be easy but nevertheless provide that we have not irrevocably violated other expectations. Unnecessary gambles with the future are unacceptable.

The United States does not meet many of these expectations. Although the U.S. economy is said to be private, free enterprise, and capitalist, in fact it is one in which the government is active in establishing and enforcing the rules of the game, legislating taxation, supporting R&D, providing public goods, and the like. Corporate power distorts, informs, even can control markets. Thus to suppose that we live in a private, capitalist utopia (or dystopia) would be absurd. Yet repeatedly we are told, and shown, that indeed we live in such a counterfactual economy.

Modifications to the present system could possibly achieve more of our expectations than now exist. Whether it is even feasible to work through our current policy to achieve incremental but meaningful change is another question, if only because of the power invested in confounding and eroding democratic change by often inimical power. Further, politics and economics must be considered globally, for that is the current reality and both are increasingly moving in that direction. Indeed, many opacities in our social policy profit by global illumination. However, certain social policy issues must remain local or national. Appealing to some abstract globalism as a reason for local and national inaction and cynicism is fraudulent.

Many conceivable alternatives to capitalism exist—historically, feudalism, hunter-gatherer economies, slavery, and so on, and today, corporate bureaucracies, families, institutions of altruism, and the like. And let us not leave out socialism. Socialism presents the most attractive democratic alternative to capitalism, one that promises a furtherance of decent expectations.

By socialism is meant a system of economic democracy in which production is not controlled by the wealthy and the powerful, the haves, but rather by those who produce, the workers, the economic citizens.

Karl Marx believed he had discovered a scientific socialism. Even using the broader German word for science, *Wissenschaft*, in hindsight socialism is neither scientific[12] nor inevitable. Rather, it is ethical and political. The alternatives of utopian socialism are provocative, if sometimes bizarre, yet they contain an ethical and political truth: neither capitalism nor socialism is inevitable. Systems supposedly predicated in greater or lesser part on ostensible inevitability as Lenin, Stalin, and Mao professed, while furthering some of the expectations cited earlier, have destroyed others with disastrous effects, such as economic inefficiency, the purges, and the Gulag.[13]

Whether such doctrines and regimes failed or changed because of outside pressure, technological change, globalism, or other factors will not be decided here. These forms of socialism were not democratic; indeed, they were inherently antidemocratic. Partly to prevent the perversions that have characterized much that is called socialist, partly for reasons that have to do with the practicalities of getting from here to there, and partly because democracy is a good thing, the socialism advanced here is democratic socialism. The modifier "democratic" is used in two senses: first, to describe the process of getting from here to there, and, second, to describe the goal. Both the process and the goal must be democratic. It is important to note that "democratic" here does not mean restricting political activity to often meaningless votes in increasingly corpocratically rigged elections. Although there are times and places where voting and getting other people to vote is vital, the term "democratic" here means using such mechanisms of democracy as community organization, genuine participation, skillful use of power, education, reason, and so on.

In theory, some of the expectations cited earlier may be possible within capitalism. As has been suggested, if the tendency toward inequality in income and wealth is inherent in capitalism, its practical effects could be reduced by progressive income taxes, increased taxes on the wealthy, inheritance taxes, and capital gains taxes. Pollution and environmental exploitation could be reduced by regulation or fines. Other obnoxious behavior could also be reduced. Establishing appropriate taxes and regulations is a complex undertaking, but no more complex than many undertakings routine to our political economy.

However, nothing of the sort happens. Inequality only increases. Increasing, too, are proclamations claiming that taxation is unjust, confiscatory, and harmful. Moreover, the considerable resources diverted to maintaining the status quo are only increasing its distance from our expectations by expensive and talented lawyers, public-relations firms, and lobbyists. Taxation could achieve the expectations described earlier only under a different dispersion of power whereby haves, business, corporations, and other constituents of a corpocracy did not possess overwhelming power. Thus taxation is only a theoretical, utopian, impractical, and abstract remedy presupposing changes in the polity that can be realized only by more fundamental change in the political economy.

Often, in economic arguments, efficiency and equity are set at odds. The arguments leave something to be desired. Yet inefficiency is an economic perversion, meaning, inter alia, waste, corruption, and misallocation of resources. Efficiency is as legitimate as the other expectations listed earlier. At least in the short term, economic efficiency may result from markets that work, but that is insufficient justification for them. Indeed, the question is not simply markets or no markets. It is far more complex. When, where, and how are markets useful, and when, where, and how are they to be regulated and controlled? How can global markets be democratically controlled? When, where, and how are markets constructed? When, where, and how are the multitudinous relationships that exist among people properly commodities on markets?

Markets have a place in a decent society if they serve the people. A society in which people serve markets is routinely open to injustice, particularly when markets are controlled by giant capitalist corporations. Indeed, markets are a particularly convenient way for corporations to justify their control of organizations and people. Even if valuable, markets must be subject to intense and continual scrutiny in the democracy advocated here. All this is true not only of nations but of the entire planet.

Efficiency in a democratic socialist economy may be achieved in a number of ways, none of which are through centralized decision making, price setting, or job description, and all of which gave some earlier socialist governments excessive power by combining control of work, goods, and consumption under traditional centralized control. One way to achieve efficiency is by computerized economic models. An example might be Wassily Leontief's linear input–output analysis, although the Leontief matrix may be nonlinear.[14] But modern computers are sufficiently powerful to model the market itself. Of course, any such mechanism must be democratically controlled. Alternatively, or conjointly, democratic socialism could be market socialism[15] consisting of workers democratically controlling their firms, instead of the current case of shareholders, boards of directors, and management controlling them. Firms may interact with one another and with consumers through a market regulated to prevent monopolies and to protect the environment—in short, to do what the government should do but what is increasingly done by corporations.

Economic theory is agnostic concerning the possibility of market socialism.[16] That the organization of market socialism has not been thoroughly researched is largely a product of the current distribution of money and power. There is no reason to suspect that market socialism or computer-modeled socialism or both are any less efficient than capitalism, which is replete with its own inefficiencies, such as free riders, regulations, externalities, public goods, and destruction of the environment. Further, there is no reason for market socialism to be concerned only with the here and now. Clearly the economy affects the future, and development must be sustainable.

Still other forms of political economy are possible. The political economy of the family could be different from what it is today, perhaps less patriarchal. It will not be capitalist, nor will it rely on the domination of women, the poverty of children, or the exploitation of have-nots. New forms of communes and collectives may exist in this future along with market socialism. Further, market socialism may not be the ultimate form of political economy. Some other form of participatory economy may come into being. Such alternative forms could coexist with market socialism. The extent of each could be decided by radical political democracy, but our crystal ball grows foggy.

In principle, there is no reason why forms of a safety net cannot be provided under capitalism. The characteristics of this safety net involve matters we already know about, like unemployment insurance, Social Security, disability insurance, universal health care, and the like. While theoretically possible under capitalism, modern corpocratic global capitalism is bent on decreasing them, if not eliminating them altogether. The global economy and corporate demands eventuate in an assault on social policy. In part this assault issues from corporations, from their leanness and meanness; in part it derives from the requisites of neoliberal globalization and transnational competition; and in part it is a function of relatively mobile capital and immobile labor. At times, we are told there is simply not enough money.

But the amount of money available for the welfare state, economic redistribution, and social policy is a product of prior budgetary decisions that have left a disproportionate share of money to corporations, banks, insurance companies, and defense. Thus the excuse of insufficient funds cannot be accepted. Further, budgetary decisions predicated on the necessities of markets are influenced by them. Under modern global capitalism, the situation of equity and the existence of a serious safety net are too abstract to be sensible. Our expectations, however, that work not be incarcerating, that it enhance civic virtues, and that it be democratic have more to do with the organization of work than with economic considerations. Bureaucratic organization is dangerous, dominating, and antidemocratic. Moreover, bureaucracies dominate and homogenize people, who in fact have rights and are unique.

A common argument for capitalism is that the same incentives (like money) serve people, the organization, and the economy, the same holding for other incentives and disincentives such as fines, firing, and taxes. Economics used incentives and disincentives, carrots and sticks, well before psychology's lengthy flirtation with positive and negative reinforcements. This might suggest that modern behaviorism issued from economics. But such positive and negative reinforcements have been part of our common sense since the domestication of animals. It is questionable, however, whether such reinforcements are the only motivations of behavior and whether, under different social and economic arrangements, they would even approach the significance they currently have. Freud has done some of the work for us.[17] Behavior is far more complex. As to the second point, Marx offers alternatives. Modern cognitive science suggests that knowledge, language, even yearnings for freedom are part of human nature. Evolutionary psychology proposes that these qualities, and others like altruism, may be genetically influenced. All these possibilities are enough to do away with the certainty of carrots and sticks even under capitalism, never mind when we change the rules of the game or the game itself.

Socialism has been criticized for its bureaucracy. Indeed, the abuse of bureaucratic coercion comes more easily in socialism than in capitalism. But capitalism is as bureaucratic. As noted earlier, bureaucracy flourished in the United States as a way to continue private corporations beyond their original owners' deaths, as a mechanism of immortality. Bureaucracy and capitalism are not at odds. Indeed, the issue is not only socialism versus capitalism, but bureaucracy versus alternative organization, specifically nonbureaucratic democratic organization. Currently much of the internal workings of corporations is likely to be bureaucratic, authoritarian, or totalitarian. Corporate, antidemocratic, bureaucratic organization extends beyond corporations to advertising and public relations, influencing possibly such noncorporate institutions as government, schools, and charity. What constitutes radical democratic organization is as important a question as what constitutes a radically democratic economy. Indeed, since it is largely in organization that past socialisms have failed, that question is crucial.

One definition of socialism is the control of substantial parts of the economy, including significant elements of the means of production, distribution, and the safety net of the state, as exemplified by long experience with the Soviet Union, those countries subservient to it, and those emulating it. The tyranny, murder, corruption, and inefficiency of these systems is by now obvious to all, even through the distortions of rhetoric like the Evil Empire, the Red Menace, "Better dead than red," and the oratory describing "the other side." How easy it is to call such perversions nasty names, to claim they are engendering a new class, to question their ethics and sanity. Yet one cannot cast them off quite that lightly. However perversely, they did embody certain aspects of socialism as surely as the United States embodies, however imperfectly, much of what capitalism is. More equality and stronger safety nets were more common to some of these systems. Yet often freedom was inexpressible, democracy was abstract, bureaucracy went unchecked, and corruption flourished. And this does not even begin to address the horrors recounted by Arthur Koestler,[18] Aleksandr Solzhenitsyn,[19] and George Orwell.[20]

On the contrary, we envisage a radically democratic socialism wherein people have important decision-making powers in the organization of production. Many such powers are little more than the extension of powers that theorists of democracy wrote into the government of life apart from work before the organization of work became dominated by bureaucratic corporations exerting profound influence on aspects of life that do not involve work, such as school, parenting, recreation, retirement, even death. To speak of civic democracy while minimizing or neglecting the domination of corporations is to engage in abstract rhetoric. Given the power of the modern bureaucratic capitalist corporation, civic democracy is bent and corrupted.

I hope to have made a case in this book for democratic organization at work. Democracy at work looks much like other civic democracy. Hence the many existing works on civic democracy, in the Western tradition from Locke[21] to Mill,[22] are relevant to the organization of work. The problems of a polity are more complex than those of work, but more can be said specifically about work. As demonstrated by welfare economics, with some stipulations it is an abstract goal of the firm to work for the good of society. This having been said, one must immediately question what neoclassical economics means by the good of society. The answer is at hand: the good of society is neither more nor less than some aggregation of individual utility functions. Interpersonal utility comparisons are impermissible, gross disparities in wealth are permissible, and only efficiency is demanded. The good of society is not singular or a reasonable approximation of a singular end; rather, it is a collection of infinite possibilities whose only requirement is that they be on the Pareto frontier[23]—that is, that no more can be done for one person without doing less for someone else.

This is more than trivial. What guarantee do we have that a firm democratically controlled by workers would care about society at the expense of the workers involved? The answer is to be found in democratic theory not explicitly concerning work. Workers are educated in civic responsibility; they recognize their membership in a species, indeed their interdependence with people outside the firm. Citizens, unshackled both at work and off, can develop virtues like altruism, creativity, excellence, concern, even heroism and freedom. If such virtues do not seem natural, it may be because of our informal and formal education. Of course, other attributes may seem more natural, such as greed, lust, and aggression. Truly, we know very little about human nature.

One purpose of civic society is to encourage the good while discouraging the bad. This should be no less an obligation regarding the organization of work. If one of the dangers at the workplace is to act so as to maximize the interest of workers at the expense of others, attention must be paid to nourishing the good and discouraging the bad. Since people come together at their place of work, there is ample opportunity for organization toward such an end. Market virtues are perhaps sufficient to suggest that democratic socialism might significantly be market socialism. By this, I do not mean state-directed units interacting on the market. Rather, I refer to workers' democratic organizations interacting on the market (in cases where the market is an appropriate means of interaction). However, just as today's market is combined with nonmarket institutions, market socialism is to be combined with such existing nonmarket institutions as the family, as well as new nonmarket institutions that complement market socialism such as various forms of participatory economics.

Unfortunately, markets are abused in modern economies. Corporate "welfare" is a scandal. Less well recognized is the effect many provisions have in advancing free trade, much of which, originally in our Constitution and currently with respect to the global economy, is protectionist. The North American Free Trade Agreement serves to keep most of the world out of a regional market. Workers' rights, environmental decency, and sustainable development can be incorporated into global agreements. That they rarely are testifies to corporate power and a lack of global civic vision. With appropriate additions and democratic organization, a global economy is a reasonable goal. But a global economy must proceed with global democracy, and the organization of work must be an element of that global democracy. And since state power—that is, democratic civic power—is necessary to counteract corporate power, global integration of democratic organizations is a desirable and necessary complement to markets and other national and global economic arrangements.

It is a reasonable expectation for people to live together democratically and in freedom. Since one's life at work is so important, not only civic society but industrial organizations should encourage this. Unfortunately, although industrial organization is at the center of some scholarly disciplines—indeed, all disciplines if school is no more than an industry—the study and practice of industrial organization to enhance freedom and democracy is virtually nonexistent. Organization in various forms is centered on profit, efficiency, and discipline. This includes concerns with worker contentment, lack of stress, EAP programs, even a sense of democracy and freedom (terms ineloquently captured by newspeak as "input," "feedback," and "flex time"). Such endeavors are usually perceived as fraudulent by workers, who resent the time and pretense involved in participating in them.

It is understandable that research on industrial organization, directly and indirectly sponsored by employers, has as its goal the needs of employers, corporations, and bureaucracy. But since industrial organization of, by, and for workers is of paramount importance to economic freedom and industrial democracy, its serious study has been neglected and is overdue. Such study need not be confined to universities; much can be done by workers at their workplace. Currently the term "flexibility" is newspeak for "moving, hiring, and firing workers." In fact, workers should be afforded more flexibility—in its true sense—for practical experimentation in organizing their work lives. This requires a socialism in which firms governed by workers have an interest in democracy and freedom, even in exporting successful organizational ideas to other firms.

A change from capitalism to socialism is not inevitable. Nor will it be easy. It is difficult to envision corporations handing their resources over to workers. The realities of modern power linger. And, as Georges Sorel reminds us, violence is detestable, requiring organization, brutality, and bureaucracy.[24] Rarely has it proved possible to do away with such organization. Even putting aside issues of morality, violence is simply not an option in a corporate bureaucratic setting with a professional army and police well prepared to work together, having the technological spinoff of surveillance at their fingertips.

Democratic socialism should be less a means of state control than a means of democratic workers' control over their work and time at work.[25] What is to induce the transfer of capital from corporations to workers? This is a profound question. The organization, brutality, and violence involved in some past revolutions is not auspicious for the future of democracy. Yet the future is not the past.

Indeed, the reverse of the transition to socialism occurred with the conversion to private ownership in countries once socialist. This, too, involves agonies, pressures from the outside, corruption, and takeover by party hacks. Conversion in Eastern Europe was facilitated by the Soviet Union's calculation that hanging on would be painful. Conversion in the former Soviet Union is more complex. Perhaps socialism in one land was impossible, the outside pressures too great. Nationalism has reasserted itself in the Soviet Union, as in Eastern Europe, opening the possibility of an autocratic violent future. Whatever the case, it is now generally recognized that privatization in the Soviet Union is not automatic, inevitable, or magical. Much the same applies to conversion from private to public control.

In the interim, what is to be done? Options toward the progressive side of capitalism should be supported, such as strengthening unions, legislating meaningful campaign-finance reform, applying progressive pressures, and resisting commercial and military pressure directed at weaker countries. Further, one should view incremental change in the context of systemic change. Another option is conservative. Effort should be directed at preventing the privatization of the public. Thus schools, Social Security, Medicare, and some railways should remain in the public sector. Although privatization in the past twenty years has increased vastly, a significant portion of our assets are still public and ought not to slip into private hands. Conserving the status quo, when appropriate, is a priority. Public subsidization of private research should stop.

There is ample space for global action. To leave globalization to haves, transnational corporations, and nondemocratic governments is to abandon democracy, the people, and the planet. It is to ignore that we all have a democratic stake in the future of our environment. Flows of international capital should be diminished by taxation. Equality, the people, and the planet must figure in international discussion. International agreements on global trade, government, and the environment should be debated in public forums, which should be democratic. Decisions must be made regarding which resources are to be market commodities and which are not, and regarding market regulations. Excessive speculation must stop; other countries and the United States must establish mechanisms for controlling economies and markets. Corporate power must be tamed, preferably, as suggested earlier, by democratically governing corporations themselves, by economic democracy. This is particularly important as corporations leap over national borders and beyond national control. Peace, security, and respect must be ensured. The earth, the forests, the oceans, the atmosphere cannot be regarded as mere resources. These one-time gifts are far too important to be subject to corporate greed, the rich, and the powerful. Organizing the world's governments to meet these criteria and more will be difficult, of course, but surely democratic socialism in the United States would facilitate global organizational change. The history of the twentieth century has certainly shown the importance of and necessity for such global organizations.

Opportunities for organization in the community, on the job, and over the Internet exceed those working to organize. Often, organizational successes in one locality can be communicated to another and replicated according to the concrete needs of people in different situations. This makes local organization all the more important. More needs to be done than there are doers. In some measure, this is a consequence of the public-relations success that has made individual advancement, capitalism, despair, and acceptance endemic. "Lemon socialism," wherein firms that are not working are turned over to the public sector, should be regarded not as a public burden but as a possible opportunity, as should public goods and other enterprises that the private sector wants to make public. Rarely does it make sense for the government to bail out private enterprise, as was the case with the savings and loans and with Chrysler. Rather, these are occasions to make all or part of such enterprises public.

In its policy, the United States currently encourages privatization in countries where ownership had been public. Often this means the expropriation of enterprises by party hacks, by robbers become robber barons, or by "mafias." Privatization ought not to be encouraged where it has not occurred, not here or in other countries. Nor should privatization be thought of as the handmaiden of democracy, as is often the case in the World Bank, the World Trade Organization, and the International Monetary Fund. The current situation whereby decisions in these forums are predominantly controlled by the United States, and to a lesser extent by Europe and Japan, and by transnational corporate power is unjust. Global economic organization should be coupled with global democratic political organization.

Because the United States plays such a significant role in the global economy, these issues should be topics for discussion at the dinner table and the workplace. Their current absence or distortion is a scandalous victory for corpocratic public relations. Local organization and national agendas should give such issues the importance they merit.

The choice is not between socialism and markets. One can facilitate the other. A combination may make our expectations more realizable. Experience has taught us that the concentrations of power existing under capitalism grotesquely distort markets for the benefit of haves and to the detriment of have-nots. Market socialism is one appropriate vehicle for the realization of democratic change. This does not rule out alternatives, such as participatory economics. Indeed, the two might complement each other. Moreover, this does not preclude working against organizational inhumanities issuing from modern capitalism like pollution, poverty, starvation, disease, even decency and freedom. And just as socialism is not inevitable, we should not delude ourselves that it does not have visible problems like agency and lack of traditional incentives, and possible abuses like those that occurred in the Soviet Union, as well as unforeseen problems.

Democratic change is intelligent, compassionate, and nonviolent. The expectations voiced here are legitimate. The concept of human nature that informs current political and economic organization is unproven, perfidious, even vile. The changes proposed here are ones for which we should strive. Since the future, of course, is unwritten, current political activity may well create unexpected possibilities for the future. Thus there is ample reason for serious study not biased toward corporations of democratic and industrial organization, market socialism, economic information and understanding, power and politics, globalization, and social policy. Yet such study, however necessary, is an insufficient condition for democratic change.

Democratic change demands that thought be connected to action and action to thought. Usually, practical action requires that people organize around particular issues. Issues often require new thought and action. Even action around seemingly isolated issues may well require novel thought open to such realities as corporate globalization and to such possibilites as democratic change. Education for such change must be a changed education. Unfortunately, time is of the essence.

Not only is a global corpocracy harmful to people, but it may well be destroying the Earth, which is our home. We pollute the environment in which we live. Economic development under a corpocratically directed market will be sustainable only by luck. The Bush administration's rejection of the Kyoto environmental accords not only betrayed a self-righteous exceptionalism masking a conviction that might makes right, but was an authentic contribution to a more difficult future. Further, some decisions made now may lead to irreversible consequences. Many issues are not short term, and some are important while others are vital. Thus issues around which people organize must be chosen with care. Clarity, as well as thought, is required in social action. Clarity is also essential in deciding whether an issue is local, national, global, or some combination (to speak only of geographical distinctions). Often local action should be informed by global thought. But occasions do exist when civic action should be confined largely within national borders, even within particular communities. The entire globe is not always involved, and much action should properly occur in our own backyards. It is important that global, national, and local social action be guided by social knowledge and thought. Global forces will increasingly affect present and future social policy. Finally, it is imperative that we consider, discuss, and act on global governance and democracy.

# Notes

## 1. Policy

1. John H. Schaar, *Legitimacy in the Modern State* (New Brunswick, N.J.: Transaction, 1981).
2. Max Weber, Edward Shils, and Max Rheinstein, *Max Weber on Law in Economy and Society*, 2d ed., ed. Max Rheinstein (Cambridge, Mass.: Harvard University Press, 1954).
3. Robert A. Dahl, *Modern Political Analysis*, 4th ed. (Englewood Cliffs, N.J.: Prentice Hall, 1984), and *Who Governs? Democracy and Power in an American City* (New Haven, Conn.: Yale University Press, 1961).
4. C. Douglas Lummis, *Radical Democracy* (Ithaca, N.Y.: Cornell University Press, 1996).
5. Michel Foucault, *Power/Knowledge: Selected Interviews and Other Writings, 1972–1977* (New York: Pantheon, 1980), and *The History of Sexuality* (New York: Vintage, 1988).
6. Dahl, *Who Governs?*
7. Harold D. Lasswell, *Power and Society: A Framework for Political Inquiry* (New Haven, Conn.: Yale University Press, 1950).
8. Foucault, *Power/Knowledge*; *History of Sexuality*; and *Discipline and Punish: The Birth of the Prison* (New York: Pantheon, 1977).
9. Jacques Ellul, *Propaganda: The Formation of Men's Attitudes* (New York: Knopf, 1965); Edward S. Herman, *Manufacturing Consent: The Political Economy of the Mass Media* (New York: Pantheon, 1988).
10. Pierre Bourdieu, *On Television* (New York: New Press, 1998).
11. Jonathan Kozol, *Amazing Grace: The Lives of Children and the Conscience of a Nation* (New York: Crown, 1995).

12. Richard H. de Lone, *Small Futures: Children, Inequality, and the Limits of Liberal Reform* (New York: Harcourt Brace Jovanovich, 1979).
13. Joseph E. Stiglitz, *Whither Socialism?* (Cambridge, Mass.: MIT Press, 1994).
14. George Orwell, *1984* (San Diego: Harcourt Brace Jovanovich, 1984 [1977]).
15. Karl Polanyi, *Primitive, Archaic, and Modern Economies: Essays of Karl Polanyi* (Boston: Beacon Press, 1971 [1968]), and *The Great Transformation* (Boston: Beacon Press, 1957 [1944]).
16. Friedrich A. von Hayek, *The Road to Serfdom* (Chicago: University of Chicago Press, 1944), and *The Fortunes of Liberalism: Essays on Austrian Economics and the Ideal of Freedom* (Chicago: University of Chicago Press, 1992).
17. Polanyi, *Great Transformation*.
18. Stiglitz, *Whither Socialism?*; Charles E. Lindblom, *Politics and Markets: The World's Political Economic Systems* (New York: Basic Books, 1977).
19. John M. Keynes, *The General Theory of Employment, Interest, and Money* (New York: Harcourt, Brace & World, 1964).
20. Jacques Donzelot, *The Policing of Families* (New York: Pantheon, 1979).
21. George F. Gilder, *Wealth and Poverty* (New York: Basic Books, 1981).
22. John Ehrenreich, *The Altruistic Imagination: A History of Social Work and Social Policy in the United States* (Ithaca, N.Y.: Cornell University Press, 1985).
23. Foucault, *History of Sexuality*.
24. Ibid., and *Discipline and Punish*.
25. Noam Chomsky and Edward S. Herman, *Manufacturing Consent: The Political Economy of the Mass Media* (New York: Pantheon, 1988).
26. Anthony Downs, *An Economic Theory of Democracy* (New York: Harper, 1957).

## 2. Corporations

1. Charles E. Lindblom, *Politics and Markets: The World's Political Economic Systems* (New York: Basic Books, 1977).
2. Gerard Debreu, *Theory of Value: An Axiomatic Analysis of Economic Equilibrium* (New Haven, Conn.: Yale University Press, 1959).
3. Oskar Morgenstern, *Selected Economic Writings of Oskar Morgenstern* (New York: New York University Press, 1976).
4. John K. Galbraith, *American Capitalism: The Concept of Countervailing Power*, rev. ed. (Boston: Houghton Mifflin, 1956).
5. Robert J. Lifton, *Revolutionary Immortality: Mao Tse-tung and the Chinese Cultural Revolution* (New York: Random House, 1968).
6. Rosabeth M. Kanter, *Men and Women of the Corporation* (New York: Basic Books, 1977).
7. Noam Chomsky, *Profit over People: Neoliberalilsm and Global Order* (New York: Seven Stories Press, 1999).
8. *Boston Globe*, July 8, 1996.

9. Lester C. Thurow, *The Zero-Sum Society: Distribution and the Possibilities for Economic Change* (New York: Basic Books, 1980).
10. Lindblom, *Politics and Markets*.
11. John M. Keynes, *The Economic Consequences of the Peace* (New York: Penguin, 1988).
12. Bagdish N. Bhagwati, *Income Taxation and International Mobility* (Cambridge, Mass.: MIT Press, 1989).
13. Norbert Walker, "Europe Gets Back in Gear," *New York Times*, August 4, 1999.
14. Noam Chomsky, *Year 501: The Conquest Continues* (Boston: South End Press, 1993).
15. Max Weber, *From Max Weber: Essays in Sociology*, trans. and ed. H. H. Gerth and C. Wright Mills (New York: Oxford University Press, 1946), and *The Protestant Ethic and the Spirit of Capitalism* (London: Allen & Unwin, 1930).
16. Dani Rodrik, *Has Globalization Gone Too Far?* (Washington, D.C.: Institute for International Economics, 1997).
17. Thomas Hobbes, *Leviathan* (Harmondsworth: Penguin, 1968).
18. Paul Krugman, *The Return of Depression Economics* (New York: Norton, 1999).

## 3. Poverty

1. United Nations Development Programme, "Human Development Report," 1999, available at http://www.undp.org/hdro/index2.html.
2. Bradley R. Schiller, *The Economics of Poverty and Discrimination*, 6th ed. (Englewood Cliffs, N.J.: Prentice Hall, 1995).
3. Ibid.
4. Richard H. de Lone, *Small Futures: Children, Inequality, and the Limits of Liberal Reform* (New York: Harcourt Brace Jovanovich, 1979).
5. Talcott Parsons, *The Social System* (Glencoe, Ill.: Free Press, 1951).
6. Karl Marx, *Capital* (New York: Dutton, 1957).
7. Jonathan Kozol, *Amazing Grace: The Lives of Children and the Conscience of a Nation* (New York: Crown, 1995).
8. Kevin P. Phillips, *The Politics of Rich and Poor: Wealth and the American Electorate in the Reagan Aftermath* (New York: Harper Perennial, 1991).
9. George F. Gilder, *Wealth and Poverty* (New York: Basic Books, 1981).
10. Richard J. Herrnstein and Charles A. Murray, *The Bell Curve: Intelligence and Class Structure in American Life* (New York: Free Press, 1994).
11. Stephen J. Gould, *The Mismeasure of Man*, rev. and exp. ed. (New York: Norton, 1996).
12. Jean-Paul Sartre, *Anti-Semite and Jew* (New York: Schocken, 1948).
13. Schiller, *Economics of Poverty and Discrimination*.
14. See discussion papers from the Institute for Research on Poverty, Madison, Wisconsin.

15. John H. Ehrenreich, *The Altruistic Imagination: A History of Social Work and Social Policy in the United States* (Ithaca, N.Y.: Cornell University Press, 1985).

16. "Insurers Spend Millions for Influence," *Best's Review* (Property/Causality Insurance ed.) 9, no. 1 (1999): 16.

17. "Plan of Attack: Why Do Corporations Pay $500-an-Hour-and-Up Fees to Beltway Lobbyists?" *Mother Jones*, July 1998, 28.

18. "Not-So-Strange Bedfellows: Congressional Committees Influenced by Special Interest Groups," *Business Week*, January 25, 1999, 32.

19. Juliana Gruenwald, "Hoping to Fend Off Regulation, High-Tech Industry Steps Up Its Campaign Contributions," *Congressional Quarterly Weekly Report*, October 31, 1998, 2958.

20. Michael Rust and Jennifer G Hickey, "When Money Talks," *Insight on the News*, July 27, 1998, 8.

21. Burton A. Weisbrod, *The Nonprofit Economy* (Cambridge, Mass.: Harvard University Press, 1988).

22. Charles E. Lindblom, *Politics and Markets: The World's Political Economic Systems* (New York: Basic Books, 1977).

23. *Rebel Without a Cause*, dir. Nicholas Ray (Burbank, Calif.: Warner Home Video, 1983), videocassette.

24. Aaron B. Wildavsky, *The Politics of the Budgetary Process*, 4th ed. (Boston: Little, Brown, 1984).

25. Allan Sloan, "Corporate Charity: No More Business as Usual," *Business and Society Review* 2, no. 98 (1996): 30.

26. Max Weber, *From Max Weber: Essays in Sociology*, trans. and ed. H. H. Gerth and C. Wright Mills (New York: Oxford University Press, 1946).

### 4. Welfare

1. Michael B. Katz, *The Undeserving Poor: From the War on Poverty to the War on Welfare* (New York: Pantheon, 1989).

2. Deborah A. Stone, *The Disabled State* (Philadelphia: Temple University Press, 1984).

3. Jonathan Kozol, *Amazing Grace: The Lives of Children and the Conscience of a Nation* (New York: Crown, 1995).

4. George F. Gilder, *Wealth and Poverty* (New York: Basic Books, 1981).

5. Kevin P. Phillips, *The Politics of Rich and Poor: Wealth and the American Electorate in the Reagan Aftermath* (New York: Harper Perennial, 1991).

6. *New York Times*, August 10, 1999.

7. Aaron B. Wildavsky, *The Politics of the Budgetary Process* (Boston: Little, Brown, 1984).

8. Harold Watts, *Income Maintenance and Labor Supply: Econometric Studies* (New York: Academic Press, 1973).

9. Vincent J. Burke and Vee Burke, *Nixon's Good Deed: Welfare Reform* (New York: Columbia University Press, 1974).

10. Harry R. Haldeman, *The Haldeman Diaries: Inside the Nixon White House* (New York: Putnam, 1994).

11. Peter Edelman, "The Worst Thing Bill Clinton Has Done," *Atlantic Monthly*, March 1997, 43–58.

12. Richard H. de Lone, personal communication.

13. Karl R. Popper, *The Open Society and Its Enemies*, 5th ed. (Princeton, N.J.: Princeton University Press, 1966).

14. Edelman, "Worst Thing Bill Clinton Has Done."

15. Anthony Downs, *An Economic Theory of Democracy* (New York: Harper, 1957).

16. Burrhus F. Skinner, *Beyond Freedom and Dignity* (New York: Bantam, 1972).

17. Michel Foucault, *Discipline and Punish: The Birth of the Prison* (New York: Pantheon, 1977).

18. Isabel V. Sawhill, ed., *Welfare Reform: An Analysis of the Issues* (Washington, D.C.: Urban Institute, 1995).

## 5. Disability

1. Richard K. Scotch, *From Good Will to Civil Rights: Transforming Federal Disability Policy* (Philadelphia: Temple University Press, 1984).

2. Deborah A. Stone, *The Disabled State* (Philadelphia: Temple University Press, 1984).

3. Seymour B. Sarason and John Doris, *Educational Handicap, Public Policy, and Social History: A Broadened Perspective on Mental Retardation* (New York: Free Press, 1979).

4. Karl Polanyi, *The Great Transformation* (Boston: Beacon Press, 1957 [1944]).

5. Max Weber, *From Max Weber: Essays in Sociology*, trans. and ed. H. H. Gerth and C. Wright Mills (New York: Oxford University Press, 1946).

6. Available at http://www.raggededgemag.com/extra/edgextracourt2.htm.

7. John Gliedman and William Roth, *The Unexpected Minority: Handicapped Children in America* (New York: Harcourt Brace Jovanovich, 1980).

8. Ibid.

9. William Roth, *Personal Computers for Persons with Disabilities: An Analysis, with Directories of Vendors and Organizations* (Jefferson, N.C.: McFarland, 1992).

10. William Roth and Richard Sugarman, "The Phenomenology of Disability: Implications for Vocational Rehabilitation," *Rehabilitation Literature*, November–December 1984.

11. David T. Mitchell and Sharon L. Snyder, *The Body and Physical Difference: Discourses of Disability* (Ann Arbor: University of Michigan Press, 1997).
12. Richard Morfopoulous and William Roth, "Job Analysis and the Americans with Disabilities Act," *Business Horizons* 39, no. 6 (1996).
13. Stone, *Disabled State*, 1984.
14. Rosemarie G. Thomson, *Freakery: Cultural Spectacles of the Extraordinary Body* (New York: New York University Press, 1996); Mitchell and Snyder, *Body and Physical Difference*.
15. Paul Longmore, child telethons.
16. Ibid.
17. Erving Goffman, *Stigma: Notes on the Management of Spoiled Identity* (New York: Simon and Schuster, 1986).
18. Gary S. Becker, *Human Capital: A Theoretical and Empirical Analysis, with Special Reference to Education*, 3rd ed. (Chicago: University of Chicago Press, 1993).
19. *New York Times*, August 9, 1999.

## 7. Health

1. Michel Foucault, *The Birth of the Clinic: An Archaeology of Medical Perception* (New York: Vintage, 1994).
2. Available at www.ornl.gov/hgmis/project/timeline.html.
3. Lewis Thomas, *The Lives of a Cell: Notes of a Biology Watcher* (New York: Penguin, 1978).
4. Victor R. Fuchs, *Who Shall Live? Health, Economics, and Social Choice* (New York: Basic Books, 1975).
5. Judith Feder and Marilyn Moon, "Can Medicare Survive Its Saviors?" *American Prospect* (May–June 1999).
6. "Medline," 1999, available at http://www.ncbi.nlm.nih.gov/PubMed.
7. Robert J. Lifton, *The Nazi Doctors: Medical Killing and the Psychology of Genocide* (New York: Basic Books, 1986).
8. Foucault, *Birth of the Clinic*.
9. David U. Himmelstein and Steffie Woolhandler, "Why the U.S. Needs a Single Payer Health System," *Physicians for a National Health Program*, June 3, 1999, available at http://www.pnhp.org/main/SINGLE.HTML.
10. Ivan Illich, *Medical Nemesis: The Expropriation of Health* (New York: Pantheon, 1976).
11. Ibid.; Foucault, *Birth of the Clinic*.
12. Barbara Ehrenreich and John Ehrenreich, *The American Health Empire: Power, Profits, and Politics* (New York: Vintage, 1971).
13. Charles E. Lindblom, *Politics and Markets: The World's Political Economic Systems* (New York: Basic Books, 1977).

14. Daniel J. Kevles and Leroy Hood, *The Code of Codes: Scientific and Social Issues in the Human Genome Project* (Cambridge, Mass.: Harvard University Press, 1992).
15. Boston Women's Health Book Collective, *The New Our Bodies, Ourselves: A Book by and for Women* (New York: Simon and Schuster, 1996).

## 8. Children

1. Philippe Ariès, *Centuries of Childhood: A Social History of Family Life* (New York: Vintage, 1962).
2. William J. Goode, *The Family* (Englewood Cliffs, N.J.: Prentice Hall, 1982).
3. Friedrich Engels, *The Origin of the Family, Private Property, and the State* (New York: International, 1972).
4. Jacques Donzelot, *The Policing of Families* (New York: Pantheon, 1979).
5. Christopher Lasch, *Haven in a Heartless World: The Family Besieged* (New York: Basic Books, 1977).
6. Gary S. Becker, *A Treatise of the Family* (Cambridge, Mass.: Harvard University Press, 1991).
7. Elijah Anderson, *Code of the Street: Decency, Violence, and the Moral Life of the Inner City* (New York: Norton, 1999).
8. Robert H. Frank, *Luxury Fever: Why Money Fails to Satisfy in an Era of Excess* (New York: Free Press, 1999).
9. Judith L. Herman, *Trauma and Recovery* (New York: Basic Books, 1992).

## 9. Outsiders

1. William F. Whyte, *Street Corner Society: The Social Structure of an Italian Slum*, 4th ed. (Chicago: University of Chicago Press, 1993).
2. Wilfrid Sellars, *Science, Perception, and Reality* (New York: Humanities Press, 1963).
3. Robert A. Dahl, *Who Governs? Democracy and Power in an American City* (New Haven, Conn.: Yale University Press, 1961).
4. Frederick J. Turner, *The Frontier in American History* (New York: Dover, 1996).
5. Louis Hartz, *The Liberal Tradition in America* (San Diego: Harcourt Brace Jovanovich, 1991).
6. Seymour M. Lipset, *The First New Nation: The United States in Historical and Comparative Perspective* (New York: Norton, 1979).
7. David M. Potter, *People of Plenty: Economic Abundance and the American Character* (Chicago: University of Chicago Press, 1954).
8. William Roth, "Where Have You Gone, My Darling Clementine?" *Film Culture*, nos. 63–64 (1976).

9. Alexander Hamilton, John Jay, and James Madison, *The Federalist Papers*, ed. Andrew Hacker (New York: Washington Square Press, 1964).
10. Deborah A. Stone, *The Disabled State* (Philadelphia: Temple University Press, 1984).
11. *New York Times*, March 5, 1998.
12. Department of Justice, Bureau of Justice Statistics, press release, July 11, 1999.
13. *New York Times*, July 12, 1999.
14. American Psychiatric Association, *Diagnostic and Statistical Manual of Mental Disorders*, 4th ed., Text Revision (Washington, D.C.: American Psychiatric Association, 2000).
15. *New York Times*, June 12, 1999.
16. Ibid.
17. Ibid.
18. *New York Times*, March 5, 1998.
19. Michel Foucault, *Discipline and Punish: The Birth of the Prison* (New York: Pantheon, 1977).
20. Malise Ruthven, *Torture: The Grand Conspiracy* (London: Weidenfeld and Nicolson, 1978).
21. Frances F. Piven and Richard A. Cloward, *Regulating the Poor: The Functions of Public Welfare*, rev. ed. (New York: Vintage, 1993).
22. *San Francisco Bay Guardian*, March 10, 1999.
23. *New York Times*, July 13, 1999.

## 10. Democratic Change

1. C. Douglas Lummis, *Radical Democracy* (Ithaca, N.Y.: Cornell University Press, 1996).
2. A. V. Bakunin, quoted in Noam Chomsky, "What Is Anarchism?" *Our Generation* 8, no. 2.
3. Plato, *The Republic* (New York: Basic Books, 1968).
4. Vladimir Lenin, *Essential Works of Lenin: "What Is to Be Done?" and Other Writings*, ed. Henry M. Christman (Mineola, N.Y.: Dover, 1987).
5. Max Weber, *From Max Weber: Essays in Sociology*, trans. and ed. H. H. Gerth and C. Wright Mills (New York: Oxford University Press, 1946).
6. Stuart R. Schram, *The Political Thought of Mao Tse-tung* (New York: Praeger, 1963).
7. Pierre Bourdieu, *On Television* (New York: New Press, 1998).
8. Jacques Ellul, *Propaganda: The Formation of Men's Attitudes* (New York: Knopf, 1965).
9. Weber, *From Max Weber*.
10. Noam Chomsky, *Year 501: The Conquest Continues* (Boston: South End Press, 1993).
11. Aristotle, *Aristotle's Politics* (New York: Carlton, 1943).

12. Friedrich Engels, *Socialism: Utopian and Scientific* (New York: International, 1972).

13. Aleksandr I. Solzhenitsyn, *The Gulag Archipelago, 1918–1956: An Experiment in Literary Investigation* (New York: Harper Perennial, 1991).

14. Wassily W. Leontief, *Studies in the Structure of the American Economy: Theoretical and Empirical Explorations in Input–Output Analysis* (White Plains, N.Y.: International Arts and Sciences Press, 1976), and *Input–Output Economics*, 2nd ed. (New York: Oxford University Press, 1986).

15. John E. Roemer, *Equal Shares: Making Market Socialism Work: The Real Utopias Project*, vol. 2 (New York: Verso, 1996).

16. Joseph E. Stiglitz, *Whiter Socialism?* (Cambridge, Mass.: MIT Press, 1994).

17. Sigmund Freud, *Civilization and Its Discontents* (New York: Norton, 1989).

18. Arthur Koestler, *Darkness at Noon* (New York: Bantam, 1966 [1941]).

19. Solzhenitsyn, *Gulag Archipelago*.

20. George Orwell, *1984* (San Diego: Harcourt Brace Jovanovich, 1984 [1977]).

21. John Locke, *The Second Treatise on Government* (New York: Liberal Arts Press, 1952).

22. John S. Mill, *On Liberty* (New York: Penguin, 1985).

23. Edward J. Mishan, *Cost–Benefit Analysis*, 3rd ed. (Boston: Allen & Unwin, 1982).

24. Georges Sorel, *Reflections on Violence* (New York: Collier, 1967 [1950]).

25. Samuel Bowles, David M. Gordon, and Thomas E. Weisskopf, *After the Waste Land: A Democratic Economics for the Year 2000* (Armonk, N.Y.: Sharpe, 1990), and *Beyond the Waste Land: A Democratic Alternative to Economic Decline* (Garden City, N.Y.: Doubleday, 1983).

# Index